Ozzy Ronny Parthalan (Ed.)

Sport Club Santos Dumont

Ozzy Ronny Parthalan (Ed.)

Sport Club Santos Dumont

Salvador, Club, Dumont, Brazil, Football, Club, Bahia, Sport

VadPress

Imprint

Permission is granted to copy, distribute and/or modify this document under the terms of the GNU Free Documentation License, Version 1.2 or any later version published by the Free Software Foundation; with no Invariant Sections, with the Front-Cover Texts, and with the Back- Cover Texts. A copy of the license is included in the section entitled "GNU Free Documentation License".

All parts of this book are extracted from Wikipedia, the free encyclopedia (www.wikipedia.org).

You can get detailed informations about the authors of this collection of articles at the end of this book. The editors (Ed.) of this book are no authors. They have not modified or extended the original texts.

Pictures published in this book can be under different licences than the GNU Free Documentation License. You can get detailed informations about the authors and licences of pictures at the end of this book.

The content of this book was generated collaboratively by volunteers. Please be advised that nothing found here has necessarily been reviewed by people with the expertise required to provide you with complete, accurate or reliable information. Some information in this book maybe misleading or wrong. The Publisher does not guarantee the validity of the information found here. If you need specific advice (f.e. in fields of medical, legal, financial, or risk management questions) please contact a professional who is licensed or knowledgeable in that area.

Any brand names and product names mentioned in this book are subject to trademark, brand or patent protection and are trademarks or registered trademarks of their respective holders. The use of brand names, product names, common names, trade names, product descriptions etc. even without a particular marking in this works is in no way to be construed to mean that such names may be regarded as unrestricted in respect of trademark and brand protection legislation and could thus be used by anyone.

Cover image: www.ingimage.com
Concerning the licence of the cover image please contact ingimage.

Publisher:
VadPress is a trademark of
International Book Market Service Ltd., 17 Rue Meldrum, Beau Bassin, 1713-01 Mauritius
Email: info@bookmarketservice.com
Website: www.bookmarketservice.com

Published in 2012

Printed in: U.S.A., U.K., Germany. This book was not produced in Mauritius.

ISBN: 978-613-8-78311-4

Contents

Articles
Sport_Club_Santos_Dumont   1
Salvador,_Bahia   2
Campeonato_Baiano   28
Bahia   34
Alberto_Santos-Dumont   49
Brazil   59

References
Article Sources and Contributors   90
Image Sources, Licenses and Contributors   93

Sport_Club_Santos_Dumont

Full name	Sport Club Santos Dumont
Founded	May 3, 1904
Dissolved	1913
Ground	Estádio Campo da Pólvora, Salvador, Bahia state, Brazil (Capacity: 2,000)

Sport Club Santos Dumont, commonly known as **Santos Dumont**, was a Brazilian football club based in Salvador, Bahia state. They won the Campeonato Baiano once.

History

The club was founded on May 3, 1904, and named after the Brazilian pioneer of aviation, Alberto Santos-Dumont.[1] They won the Campeonato Baiano in 1910.[2] The club closed folded in 1913.

Achievements

- **Campeonato Baiano:**
    - **Winners (1):** 1910

Stadium

Sport Club Santos Dumont played their home games at Estádio Campo da Pólvora.[1] The stadium had a maximum capacity of 2,000 people.[1]

References

[1] Rodolfo Rodrigues (2009). *Escudos dos Times do Mundo Inteiro*. Panda Books. p. 97.
[2] *Placar Guia 2011* (1350-C): 72. January 2011.

Salvador,_Bahia

Salvador
— Municipality —
O Município do *São Salvador da Bahia de Todos os Santos* **The Municipality of the** **Saint Savior of the Bay of all Saints**

 Flag **Seal**
Nickname(s): *Capital da Alegria* (Capital of happiness), *Roma Negra* (Black Rome) and *Bahia Judia* (Jewish Bay).
Motto: *Sic illa ad arcam reversa est* (And thus the dove returned to the ark)
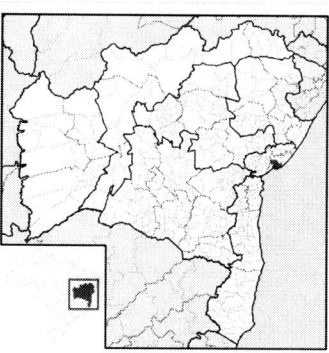 Location of Salvador in the State of Bahia

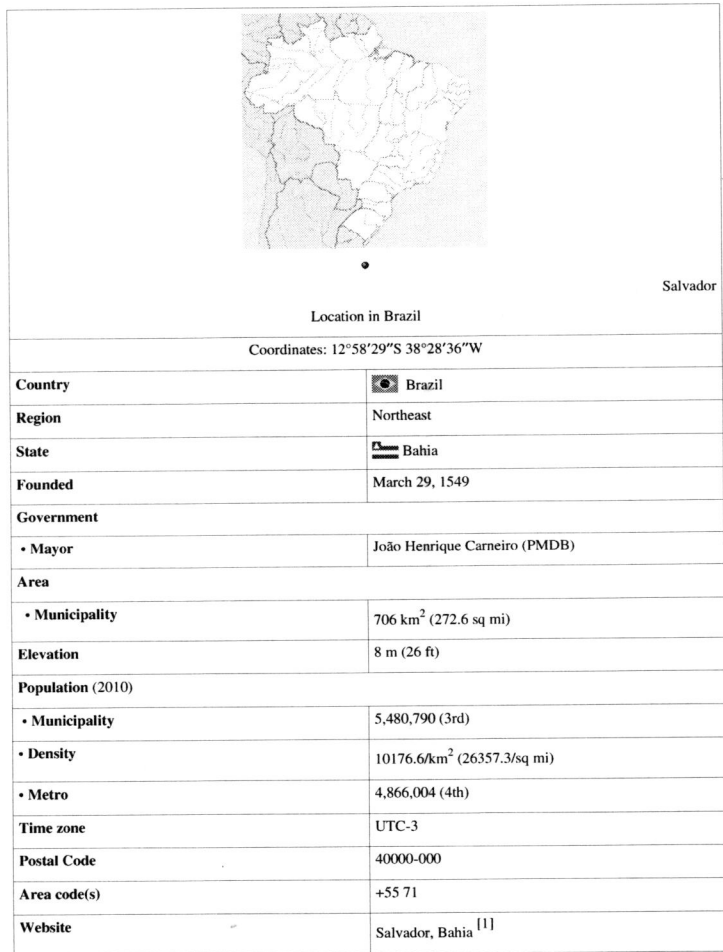

Salvador
Location in Brazil
Coordinates: 12°58′29″S 38°28′36″W

Country	Brazil
Region	Northeast
State	Bahia
Founded	March 29, 1549
Government	
• Mayor	João Henrique Carneiro (PMDB)
Area	
• Municipality	706 km^2 (272.6 sq mi)
Elevation	8 m (26 ft)
Population (2010)	
• Municipality	5,480,790 (3rd)
• Density	10176.6/km^2 (26357.3/sq mi)
• Metro	4,866,004 (4th)
Time zone	UTC-3
Postal Code	40000-000
Area code(s)	+55 71
Website	Salvador, Bahia [1]

Salvador (Portuguese pronunciation: [sawva'doʁ], *Saviour*; historic name: **Cidade de São Salvador da Bahia de Todos os Santos**, in English: "City of the Holy Saviour of the Bay of all Saints"[2] [3]) is the largest city on the northeast coast of Brazil and the capital of the Northeastern Brazilian state of Bahia. Salvador is also known as *Brazil's capital of happiness* due to its easygoing population and countless popular outdoor parties, including its street carnival. The first colonial capital of Brazil, the city is one of the oldest in the Americas. For a long time, it was simply known as **Bahia**, and appears under that name (or as *Salvador da Bahia*, *Salvador of Bahia* so as to differentiate it from other Brazilian cities of the same name) on many maps and books from before the mid-20th century. Salvador is the third most populous Brazilian city, after São Paulo and Rio de Janeiro.

The city of Salvador is notable in Brazil for its cuisine, music and architecture, and its metropolitan area is the wealthiest in Brazil's Northeast. The African influence in many cultural aspects of the city makes it the center of Afro-Brazilian culture. This reflects a situation in which African-associated cultural practices are celebrated. The historical center of Salvador, frequently called the Pelourinho, is renowned for its Portuguese colonial architecture with historical monuments dating from the 17th through the 19th centuries and was declared a World Heritage Site by UNESCO in 1985.

Salvador is located on a small, roughly triangular peninsula that separates Todos os Santos Bay from the open waters of the Atlantic Ocean. The bay, which gets its name from having been discovered on All Saints' Day forms a natural harbor. Salvador is a major export port, lying at the heart of the *Recôncavo Baiano*, a rich agricultural and industrial region encompassing the northern portion of coastal Bahia.

A particularly notable feature is the escarpment that divides Salvador into the *Cidade Alta* ("Upper Town" - rest of the city) and the *Cidade Baixa* ("Lower Town" - northwest region of the city), the former some 85 m (279 ft) above the latter,[4] with the city's cathedral and most administrative buildings standing on the higher ground. An elevator (the first installed in Brazil), known as *Elevador Lacerda*, has connected the two sections since 1873, having since undergone several upgrades.

History

Sunset and the Atlantic Ocean.

Abelardo Rodrigues Museum.

Baía de Todos os Santos (All Saints Bay) was first encountered by the Portuguese and named in 1500. In 1501, one year after the arrival of Pedro Álvares Cabral's fleet in Porto Seguro, Gaspar de Lemos arrived at Todos os Santos Bay and sailed most of the Bahia coast. But the first European man to disembark on "Morro de São Paulo," Saint Paul's Mount, was Martim Afonso de Sousa, in 1531, leading an expedition to explore the coast of the new continent.[5]

In 1510, a ship, containing the Portuguese settler named Caramuru by the natives, wrecked near the borough of Rio Vermelho. In 1534, Francisco Pereira Coutinho founded a town near Barra borough, called *Vila Velha*, Portuguese for "Old Village."[6]

In 1549, a fleet of Portuguese settlers headed by Tomé de Sousa, the first Governor-General of Brazil, established Salvador. Built on a high cliff overlooking All Saints bay as the first colonial capital of colonial Brazil, it quickly became its main sea port and an important center of the sugar industry and the slave trade.[7]

Salvador became the main entry-point for many Dutch and Jewish settlers. It was during the 17th and 19th centuries that the majority of Jews migrated to Bahia, spreading their culture throughout its colonies and beyond (the first synagogue in America, [Kahal Zur Israel Synagogue [8]], was erected in nearby Recife in 1636).

Salvador was, however, primarily influenced by Catholicism; it became the seat of the first Catholic bishopric of Brazil in 1552 and is still a center of Brazilian Catholicism. By 1583, there were 1,600 people residing in the city, and it quickly grew into one of the largest cities in the New World, surpassing any colonial American city at the time of the American Revolution in 1776.

Salvador was divided into an upper and a lower city, the upper one being the administrative and religious area and where the majority of

Hotel area of Ondina at night.

the population lived. The lower city was the financial center, with a port and market. In the late 19th Century, funiculars and an elevator, the *Elevador Lacerda*, were built to link the two areas.[9]

Salvador was the capital city of the Portuguese viceroyalty of Grão-Pará and its province of Baía de Todos os Santos. The Dutch admiral Piet Hein of the West Indian Company captured and sacked the city in May 1624, and held it along with other north east ports until it was retaken by a Spanish-Portuguese fleet in May 1625. It then played a strategically vital role in the Portuguese-Brazilian resistance against the Dutch.

Salvador was the first capital of Brazil and remained so until 1763, when it was succeeded by Rio de Janeiro. The city became a base for the Brazilian independence movement and was attacked by Portuguese troops in 1812, before being liberated on July 2, 1823. It settled into graceful decline over the next 150 years, out of the mainstream of Brazilian industrialization. It remains, however, a national cultural and tourist center. By 1948 the city had some 340,000 people, and was already Brazil's fourth largest city. In 2010 was 5,480,790 people, the third largest population of Brazil.

Campo Grande Square.

In the 1990s, a major city project cleaned up and restored the old downtown area, the *Pelourinho*, or *Centro Historico* ("Historical Center"). Now, the Pelourinho is a cultural center, and the heart of Salvador's tourist trade. Nonetheless, this social prophylaxis resulted in the forced removal of thousands of working class residents to the city's periphery where they have encountered significant economic hardship.[10]

Additionally, the Historical Center is now something of a depopulated architectural jewel whose "animation" must be brought in and sponsored by local shopowners and the Bahian state. Similar situations may be found in many UNESCO World Heritage Sites today but the Pelourinho, in light of Salvador's economic inequalities and ruling governmental coalition's of the 1990s, seems to have gone farther than most in sacrificing its population to the needs of tourist-based preservation.[11]

Climate

Salvador features a tropical rainforest climate with no discernable dry season. Temperatures are relatively constant throughout the course of the year, featuring warm and humid conditions. Salvador's driest month of the year is February, where the city receives on average 11 cm of precipitation. Salvador's wettest months are between May and July and 21 cm of rain falls during these 3 months.

Demographics

According to the 2010 IBGE Census, there were 2,480,790 people residing in the city of Salvador.[13] The census revealed the following numbers: 1,382,543 Brown (Multiracial) people (51.7%), 743,718 Black people (27.8%), 505,645 White people (18.9%), 35,785 Asian people (1.3%), 7,563 Amerindian people (0.3%).[14]

In 2010, the city of Salvador was the 3rd most populous city in Brazil, after São Paulo and Rio de Janeiro.[15]

In 2010, the city had 474,827 opposite-sex couples and 1,595 same-sex couples. The population of Salvador was 53.3% female and 46.7% male.[14]

Rio Vermelho and Horto Florestal.

Most of the population is in part descended from Black African slaves, who were mainly Yoruba speakers from Nigeria, Ghana, Togo and Benin.[16]

According to an autosomal DNA study, the ancestral heritage of the population of Salvador was estimated to be 49.20% African, 36.30% European and 14.50% Native American.[17]

Population growth

Changing demographics of the city of Salvador
Source: Planet Barsa Ltda.[18]

View of Farol da Barra Lighthouse.

The wooded Centenário Avenue.

Sunset in Plataforma Neighborhood.

Religion

Religion	Percentage	Number
Catholic	60.54%	1,479,101
No religion	18.14%	443,236
Protestant	13.29%	324,785
Spiritist	2.53%	61,833
Umbandist	1.49%	11,959
Jewish	1.03%	698
Others	4.35%	106,320

Source: IBGE 2000.[19]

Economy

Business buildings in the area of Avenida Tancredo Neves, the city's financial district.

Throughout Brazilian history Salvador has played an important role.. Throughout the colonial era Salvador was the colony's largest and most important city. Because of its location on Brazil's northeastern coast, the city served as an important link in the Portuguese empire, maintaining close commercial ties with Portugal and Portuguese colonies in Africa and Asia. Salvador remained the preeminent city in Brazil until 1763 when it was replaced as the national capital by Rio de Janeiro. In the last ten years many high-rise office and apartment buildings were constructed, sharing the same blocks with colonial-era housing or commercial buildings.[20] With its beaches, humid tropical climate, numerous up-to-date shopping malls(The Shopping Iguatemi is the first Shopping in Brazil Northeast and pleasant high-class residential areas, the city has much to offer its residents. Economically Salvador is one of Brazil's more important cities. Since its founding the city has been one of Brazil's most prominent ports and international trading centers. Boasting a large oil refinery, a petrochemical plant and other important industries, the city has made great strides in reducing its historical dependence on agriculture for its prosperity.[21]

Salvador is the second most popular tourism destination in Brazil, after Rio de Janeiro.[22] Tourism and cultural activity are important generators of employment and income, boosting the art]s and the preservation of artistic and cultural heritage. Chief among the points of interest are its famous *Pelourinho* (named after the colonial pillories that once stood there) district, its historic churches,[23] and its beaches. Salvador's tourism infrastructure is considered one of the most modern in World, especially in terms of lodging. The city offers accommodation to suit all tastes and standards, from youth hostels to international hotels. Construction is one of the most important activities in the city, and many international (mainly from Spain, Portugal and England)[24] and national developers are investing in the city and in the Bahian littoral zone.

The extreme south point.

Ford Motor Company has a plant in the Metropolitan Region of Salvador, in the city of Camaçari, assembling the Ford EcoSport, Ford Fiesta, Ford Fiesta Sedan.[25] It was the first Automotive industry in Northeastern Brazil. The industry employs 800 engineers.[26]

Shopping Center Salvador.

JAC Motors will has a plant in the Metropolitan Region of Salvador, in the city of Camaçari, the new industry will result 3,500 direct jobs and 10,000 indirect jobs, the production of 100,000 vehicles by year.[27]

In December 2001, Monsanto Company inaugurated, at the Petrochemical Pole of Camaçari, in Metropolitan Region of Salvador, the first plant of the company designed to produce raw materials for the herbicide Roundup in South America. The investment is equivalent to US$ 500 millions; US$ 350 millions were spent in this initial phase. The Camaçari Plant, the largest unit of Monsanto outside of the United States, is also the only Monsanto plant manufacturing raw materials for the Roundup production line. The company started the civil works for the new plant in January 2000.[28]

Convent and Church of São Francisco in Historic Centre.

Economy[29]	GDP (in reais)	GDP per capita (in reais)
2003	30,929,310,000	15,541
2004	47,887,968,000	18,557
2005	78,145,303,000	25,283
2006	95,072,400,000	30,870
2010	300,668,442,000	60,959

Tourism and recreation

Porto da Barra Beach.

Lacerda Elevator and Model Market in Historic Centre.

Salvador Shopping, the Brazil's largest. The shopping was elected the most modern and beautiful of South America.

The Salvador coastline is one of the longest for cities in Brazil. There are 80 km (50 mi) of beaches distributed between the High City and the Low City, from Inema, in the railroad suburb to the Praia do Flamengo, on the other side of town. While the Low City beaches are bordered by the waters of the All Saints Bay (the country's most extensive bay), the High City beaches, from Farol da Barra to Flamengo, are bordered by the Atlantic Ocean. The exception is Porto da Barra Beach, the only High City beach located in the All Saints Bay.

The big hotels tend to be strung out along the orla (Atlantic seafront). There are also smaller hotels in Barra and Porto da Barra, others (generally less expensive) scattered along the principal thoroughfare of Avenida Sete de Setembro (shortened to "Avenida Sete" by the locals), and still others (usually inexpensive) in and around Pelourinho.[30]

There are also pousadas (guest houses, or bed and breakfasts) in Barra, Pelourinho, and Santo Antônio (and other places as well, to be sure), and hostels (albergues), which are for the most part located in Pelourinho (though a lot of the "pousadas" in Barra are hostels as well).

The capital's beaches range from calm inlets, ideal for swimming, sailing, diving and underwater fishing, as well as open sea inlets with strong waves, sought by surfers. There are also beaches surrounded by reefs, forming natural pools of stone, ideal for children.

Interesting places to visit near Salvador include:

- According to the British newspaper *The Guardian*, in 2007, Porto da Barra Beach was the 3rd best in the world.[31]
- The large island of Itaparica in the Bay of All Saints can be visited either by a car-ferry, or a smaller foot-passenger ferry, which leaves from near the Mercado Modelo near the Lacerda Elevator.
- BA-099 Highway, or "Line of Coconut" and "Green Line" of towns and cities, with exquisite beaches, north of Salvador heading towards Sergipe state.
- Morro de São Paulo in the Valença region across the Bay of All Saints – an island that can be reached by ferry from Salvador (1 hour), by plane, or by bus to Valença and then by 'Rapido' ('fast') speedboat or smaller ferry. Morro de São Paulo is formed by five villages of the Tinharé Island.

The city is served by many shopping malls: Shopping Iguatemi, Salvador Shopping, Shopping Barra, and Shopping Paralela.

Salvador has four parks, green areas protected, as Jardim dos Namorados Park, Costa Azul Park, Park of the City, Park of Pituaçu.

Jardim dos Namorados is located right next to Costa Azul Park and occupies an area of 15 hectares in Pituba, where many families used to spend their vacations in the 1950s. It was inaugurated in 1969, initially as a leisure area. It underwent a complete renovation in the 1990s, with the construction of an amphitheater with room for 500 people, sports courts, playgrounds and parking for cars and tourist buses.

Costa Azul Park occupies an area of approximately 55,000 square meters, and is located in the neighborhood that goes by the same name.

Yacht Club of Bahia.

Park of the City is an important preservation area of the Atlantic forest. It was completely renovated in 2001, becoming a modern social, cultural and leisure place. The new park has 720 square meter of green area right in the middle of the city. Among the attractions are Praça das Flores (Flowers square), with more than five thousand ornamental plants and flowers. Besides its environment, the park has an infrastructure for children, with a special schedule of events taking place every October.[32]

Created by state decree in 1973, Pituaçu Park occupies an area of 450 hectares and is one of the few Brazilian ecological parks located in an urban area. It is surrounded by Atlantic forest, with a good variety of plants and animals. There is also an artificial pond in the park, built in 1906 along with the Pituaçu Dam, whose purpose was to supply water to the city. There are a number of possible leisure activities, ranging from cycloboats rides on the pond, to an 38 km (24 mi) long cycloway circling the entire reserve. Completing this infrastructure there are several options for children to play, snack bars, ice cream parlors and restrooms. A museum is also located in the park. Espaço Cravo is an outdoor museum with 800 pieces created by Mario Cravo, comprising Totems, winged and three-dimensional figures, as well as drawings and paintings.

Education

There are international schools, such as the Pan American School of Bahia. [33]

Educational institutions

The city has several universities:

- Universidade Federal da Bahia (UFBA) (Federal University of Bahia);
- Universidade Católica do Salvador (UCSal) (Catholic University of Salvador);
- Universidade do Estado da Bahia [34] (UNEB) (Bahia State University);
- Universidade Salvador [35] (UNIFACS) (Salvador University);
- Faculdade de Tecnologia e Ciências [36] (FTC) (College of Technology and Science);
- Centro Federal de Educação Tecnológica da Bahia [37] (Cefet-BA) (Federal Center of Technological Education of Bahia);
- Faculdade Ruy Barbosa [38] (FRB) (Ruy Barbosa College);
- Faculdade Castro Alves [39] (FCA) (Castro Alves College);
- Faculdade Jorge Amado [40] (FJA) (Jorge Amado College);

Callitrichidaes in the Universidade Católica do Salvador.

- Escola Bahiana de Medicina e Saúde Pública [41] (FBDC) (Bahiana College of Medicine and Public Health);
- and many others.

The city has several language schools of Portuguese for foreigners.

Primary and secondary schools

The first University of Medicine of the country, is located in Pelourinho. Nowadays it is a museum.

Top high schools of the city are Anglo-Brasileiro Academy, Federal Institute of Bahia (IFBA - Cefet), Military College of Salvador, Anchieta Academy, Oficina Academy, Salesiano Academy, Miró Academy, Marista School of Salvador, Antônio Vieira Academy, Módulo Academy, Sartre Academy, São Paulo Academy, Cândido Portinari Academy, Integral Academy, São José Academy, Alfred Nobel Academy (now owned of the Sartre Academy), Nossa Senhora da Conceição Academy, Santíssimo Sacramento Academy, Diplomata Academy, Nossa Senhora do Resgate Academy, Gregor Mendel Academy.[42]

Historic Centre

Historic Centre of Salvador da Bahia *	
UNESCO World Heritage Site	
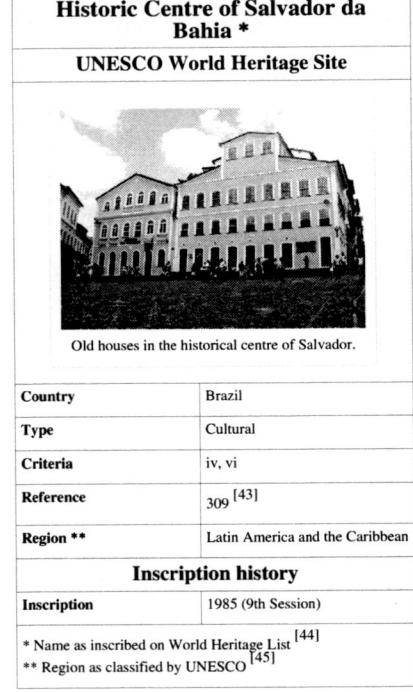	
Old houses in the historical centre of Salvador.	
Country	Brazil
Type	Cultural
Criteria	iv, vi
Reference	309 [43]
Region **	Latin America and the Caribbean
Inscription history	
Inscription	1985 (9th Session)
* Name as inscribed on World Heritage List [44] ** Region as classified by UNESCO [45]	

The Historic Centre of Salvador was designated in 1985 a World Heritage Site by UNESCO. The city represents a fine example the Portuguese urbanism from the middle of the 16th century with its higher administrative town and its lower commercial town, and a large portion of the city has retained the old character of its streets and colourful houses.

As the first capital of Portuguese America, Salvador cultivated slave labor and had its "pelourinhos" pillories installed in open places like the terreiro de Jesus and the squares know today as Thomé de Souza and Castro Alves. The "pelourinho" was a symbol of authority and justice, for some, and lashings and injustice for the majority.[46] The one erected for a short time in what is now the Historical Center, and later moved to what is now the Praça da Piedade (Square of Piety), ended up lending its name to the historical and architectural complex of Pelourinho, part of the city's historical center.

Since 1992, the Pelourinho neighborhood has been subject to a nearly US$ 100 million "restoration" that has led to the rebuilding of hundreds of buildings' facades and the expulsion of the vast majority of the neighborhood's Afro-descendent population. This process has given rise to substantial political debate in the State of Bahia, since the Pelourinho's former residents have been for the most part excluded from the renovation's economic benefits (reaped by a few). A major restoration effort resulted in making the area a highly desirable tourist attraction.[47]

Salvador's considerable wealth and status during colonial times (as capital of the colony during 250 years and which gave rise to the Pelourinho) is reflected in the magnificence of its colonial palaces, churches and convents, most of them dating from the 17th and 18th centuries. These include:

- Cathedral of Salvador: Former Jesuit church of the city, built in the second half of the 17th century. Fine example of Mannerist architecture and decoration.
- Convent and Church of São Francisco: Franciscan convent and church dating from the first half of the 18th century is another fine example of the Portuguese colonial architecture. The Baroque decoration of the church is among the finest in Brazil.
- Church of Nosso Senhor do Bonfim: Rococo church with Neoclassical inner decoration. The image of Nosso Senhor do Bonfim is the most venerated in the city, and the Feast of Our Lord of Good Ending (*Festa de Nosso Senhor do Bonfim*) in January is the most important in the city after Carnival.
- Mercado Modelo (Model Market): In 1861, at the Cayrú Square, the Customs Building was constructed, with a rotunda (large circular room with a domed ceiling) at the back end, where ships anchored to unload their merchandise. In 1971, a market began to operate in the Customs Building, and thirteen years later, it caught fire, burned down, and underwent reform. Today, there are 200 stands with a variety of arts and crafts made in Bahia as well as other states in northeastern region of Brazil, two restaurants, and several bars that serve typical drinks and appetizers.
- Elevador Lacerda (Lacerda Elevator): Inaugurated in 1873, this elevator was planned and built by the businessman Antônio Francisco de Lacerda, The four elevator cages connect the 72 metres (236 ft) between the Thomé de Souza Square in the upper city, and the Cayru Square in the lower city. In each run, which lasts for 22 seconds, the elevator transports 128 persons, 24 hours a day.

Culture

Salvador's historical and cultural aspects were inherited by the miscigenation of such ethnic groups as Native-Indian, African, European and Jewish. This mixture can be seen in the religion, golden cuisine, cultural manifestations, and custom of Bahia's people.

Literature

Fort of São Diogo.

As the capital of colonial Brazil until 1763, Salvador was an important cultural centre since the 16th century, as reflected in the large number of prominent literary figures associated with colonial Salvador, usually educated in the religious schools of the convents of the city and in the University of Coimbra in Portugal. *Frei Vicente do Salvador* (1564–1635), a Bahia-born Franciscan friar who studied in the Jesuit School of Salvador, was the author of the first book on Brazilian history written by a Brazil-born author.

Gregório de Mattos, born in Salvador in 1636, was also educated by the Jesuits. He became the most important Baroque poet in colonial Brazil for his religious and satirical works. Father António Vieira was born in Lisbon in 1608, but was raised and educated in the Jesuit school of Salvador and died in the city in 1697. His erudite sermons have earned him the title of best writer of the Portuguese language in the Baroque era.[48]

Isometric view of the Salvador Bahia Pelourinho's Anchieta Plaza, cut from a Laser Scan preservationist project conducted by nonprofit CyArk.

After the Independence of Brazil (1822), Salvador continued to play an important role in Brazilian literature. Significant 19th century writers associated with the city include Romantic poet Castro Alves (1847–1871) and diplomat Ruy Barbosa (1849–1923). In the 20th century, Bahia-born Jorge Amado (1912–2001), although not born in Salvador, helped popularize the culture of the city around the world in novels such as *Jubiabá*, *Dona Flor e Seus Dois Maridos*, and *Tenda dos Milagres*, the settings of which are in Salvador.

Religion

In Salvador, religion is a major contact point between Portuguese and African influences and, in the last 20 years, Brazil's version of a North American-influenced Pentecostalism. Salvador was the seat of the first bishopric in colonial Brazil (established 1551), and the first bishop, *Pero Fernandes Sardinha*, arrived already in 1552. The Jesuits, led by the Manuel da Nóbrega, also arrived in the 16th century and worked in converting the Indigenous peoples of the region to Roman Catholicism.

Many religious orders came to the city, following its foundation: Franciscans, Benedictines and Carmelites. Subsequently to them are created the Third Orders, the Brotherhoods, and Fraternities, which were composed mainly of professional and social groups. The most prominent of these orders were the Terceira do Carmo Order and the de São Francisco Order, founded by white men, and the Nossa Senhora do Rosário and São Beneditino Brotherhoods, composed of black men. In many churches maintained by religious men, were housed the Santíssimo Sacramento brotherhoods.

Besides these organizations, the expansion of Catholicism in the city was consolidated through social care work. Santa Casa the Misericórdia was one of the institution that did this kind of work, maintaining hospitals, shelters for the poor and the elderly, as well providing assistance to convicts and to those who would face death penalties. The convents, on their part, were cultural and religious formation centers, offering seminar coursed that often were attended by the lay.

Former Jesuit church of Salvador (17th century), now cathedral.

Even with the present evolution, and the growth of Protestantism and other religions in the city, the Catholic faith remains as one of its most distinctive features, drawing a lot of people to its hundreds of churches. Some aspects, like the use of Portuguese in the Masses, the simplification of the liturgy, and the adoption of "pop" religious songs are key factors to the triumph of Catholicism. In the Nossa Senhora do Rosário dos Pretos Church, Masses are held in the Yorubá language, making use of African chants and typical clothes, which attract many people from the African Brazilian communities.

Protestant Church in Iguatemi Neighborhood.

Most enslaved Africans in Bahia were brought from Sub-Saharan Africa, especially the Yoruba-speaking nation (*Iorubá* or *Nagô* in Portuguese) from present-day Nigeria. The enslaved were forced to convert to Roman Catholicism, but their original religion, Candomblé, has survived in spite of prohibitions and persecutions. The enslaved Africans managed to preserve their religion by attributing the names and characteristics of their Candomblé deities to Catholic saints with similar qualities.

Hence, as former pagan Christians once associated Pagan deities with the saints, enslaved Africans in Bahia transformed their faiths into a syncretic form of religion that still attempts to please both their own roots and the faith imposed by their masters and those caught in between both traditions. Thus, up to today, even nominal Catholics take part in Candomblé rituals in the *terreiros* or "centros". Candomblé is based on the cult of the Orishas (*Orixás*), like Obatala (*Oxalá*), father of humankind; Ogoun (*Ogum*), god of the war and iron; Yemanja (*Iemanjá*), goddess of the sea, rivers and lakes.

These religious entities have been syncretised with some Catholic entities. For instance, Salvador's Feast of Bonfim, celebrated in January, is dedicated to both Our Lord of Bonfim (Jesus Christ) and

Oxalá. Another important feast is the Feast de Yemanja every February 2, on the shores of the borough of Rio Vermelho in Salvador, on the day the church celebrates Our Lady of the Navigators. December 8, Immaculate Conception Day for Catholics, is also commonly dedicated to Yemanja' with votive offerings made in the sea throughout the Brazilian coast.

Perspective of the Cross and Church of São Francisco in Anchieta Plaza, Pelourinho, created from a Laser Scan preservationist project conducted by nonprofit CyArk.

Religious syncretism is defined as the combination of two or more creeds. In Brazil, especially in Bahia, it came up as a solution for the slaves who were prohibited from practicing their religion, so they pretended to be worshiping catholic saints while in reality they were venerating their own deities. Hence, associating an orixá (Candoblé deity) to a catholic was a strategy used by black people to maintain their beliefs and rituals alive, while they fooled their masters, making them believe that their devotion was to the catholic saints.

Catholic Church of the Ordem Terceira de São Francisco.

The lives of catholic saints and their own physical features, portrayed on sculptures and drawings, made the identification with the orixás easier. Salvador is a city where different ethnic and cultural aspects are mixed up, but religious syncretism remains as one of its most intriguing features. Its ancient churches are a proof of the power of Catholicism, which was brought by the Portuguese and forced upon Blacks and Indigenous.

Cuisine

Feijoada with several accompaniments: rice cassava fried, crackling Orange caipirinha, among others.

The local cuisine, spicy and based on seafood (shrimp, fish), strongly relies on typically African ingredients and techniques, and is much appreciated throughout Brazil and internationally. The most typical ingredient is *azeite-de-dendê*, an oil extracted from a palm tree (*Elaeis guineensis*) brought from West Africa to Brazil during colonial times.

Using the milky coconut juice, they prepared a variety of seafood based dishes, such as Ensopados, Moquecas and Escabeche. The sugar cane bagasse was mixed with molasses and Rapadura, in the creation of coconut desserts like Cocada Branca and Preta. The remaining of the Portuguese Stew sauce was mixed with manioc flour to make a mush, which is a traditional Indian dish. In the markets of Salvador, it is possible to find stands selling typical dishes of the colonial era. In the Sete Portas Market, customers eat Mocotó on Friday nights since the 1940s, when the market was inaugurated. In the restaurants of Mercado Modelo (Model Market), Sarapatel, stews and several fried dishes are served regularly. In the São Joaquim, Santa Bárbara and São Miguel markets, there are stands selling typical food. They are also sold at stands located on the beaches, specially crab stews and oysters. The restaurants that sell typical dishes are located mostly along the coast and in Pelourinho. They prepare a wide variety of recipes that take palm tree oil.

Traditional dishes include *caruru, vatapá, acarajé, bobó-de-camarão, moqueca* baiana, and *abará*. Some of these dishes, like the acarajé and abará, are also used as offerings in Candomblé rituals. An acarajé is basically a deep-fried "bread" made from mashed beans from which the skins have been removed (reputedly feijão fradinho "black-eyed peas" but in reality almost always the less expensive brown beans so ubiquitous in Bahia). But Salvador is not only typical food. Other recipes created by the slaves were the Haussá Rice (rice and jerked beef cooked together), the Munguzá, used as offering to the Candomblé deity Oxalá (who is the father of all deities, according to the religion) pleased the matrons very much. So did the Bolinhos the Fubá, the Cuscuz (cornmeal) and the Mingau (porridge). According to Arany Santana, the Ipetê (used in the rituals to the deity Oxum) became the Shrimp Bobó (a kind of mush), and the Akará (honoring the deities Xangô and Iansã) became the world-famous Acarajé. Who comes here also has a large number of restaurants specialized on international cuisine. There also places that serve dishes from other states of Brazil, especially from Minas Gerais and the Northeast region.

Capoeira

Capoeira is a unique mix of dance and martial art of Afro-Brazilian origin, combining agile dance moves with unarmed combat techniques. Capoeira in Portuguese literally means "chicken coop." The presence of capoeira in Brazil is directly connected to the importation of African slaves by the Portuguese, and Salvador is considered the centre of origin of the modern capoeira branches.[49]. In the first half of the 20th century, Salvador-born masters Mestre Bimba and Mestre Pastinha founded capoeira schools and helped standartise and popularise the art in Brazil and the world. The practice of Capoeira was banned in 1892, though in 1937 it was made legal.[50] In recent years, Capoeira has become more international and accessible even in Salvador, with classes available in English by Brooklyn-born Monitor Feijao of Capoeira Brasil Bahia.

Capoeira in Salvador.

Museums

Salvador Historical Centre.

The artistic, cultural and social heritage of Salvador is preserved in museums. From Museu de Arte da Bahia (MAB), which is the oldest in the State, to Museu Náutico, the newest, the first capital of Brazil preserve unique pieces of history and have 345 museums.

Even so, the importance of Salvador's museums has drawn the interest of experts from Brazil and abroad. There we can find valuable pieces of religious art, ornamental items from the old manors and also objects that belonged to the old families and public figures of the state. The Arte Sacra and Abelardo Rodrigues museums are must see programs. They both have the biggest sacra art collection in the country. Another obligatory tour is to Museu de Arte da Bahia.

Museu de Arte da Bahia has paintings, Chinese porcelain, furniture and sacra images from the 17th and 18th centuries. Museu Costa Pinto has private, owned items such as, pieces of art, crystal objects, furniture from the 18th and 19th centuries, tapestry, sacra pieces and Chinese porcelain. The golden jewelry and the 27 ornamental silver buckles are the most precious in the entire collection.

Another important museum is Museu da Cidade, where many items that help to preserve the heritage of old Salvador are kept. There we can find thematic objects that belonged to public personalities in the state like dolls, orixá statues and religious images. There is also an art gallery located inside of the museums. There is also Fundação Casa de Jorge Amado, with pictures, objects and the life's stories of the author of memorable novels that portray old Bahia, like Gabriela – Cravo e Canela, Dona Flor e Seus Dois Maridos, O País do Carnaval and Tieta do Agreste.

Some churches and monasteries also have museums located in their premises. Examples of this are the Carmo da Misericórdia and São Bento Museums. After the renovation of the Forts, were created Museu Náutico, in Forte de Santo Antonio da Barra (Farol da Barra) and Museu da Comunicação, in Forte São Diogo. Other important museums that are scattered through Salvador are: Museu do Cacau, Museu geológico do Estado, Museu tempostal, Solar do Ferrão, Museu de Arte Antiga e Popular Henriqueta M Catharino, Museu Eugênio Teixeira Leal and Museu das Portas do Carmo.

Carnival/Carnaval

According to the Guinness Book of Records, the carnival or *Carnaval* of Salvador da Bahia is the biggest party on the planet. For an entire week, almost 4 million people celebrate throughout 25 kilometers (16 mi) of streets, avenues and squares. The direct organization of the party involves the participation of 100 thousand people.[51] Its dimensions are gigantic. Salvador receives an average of 800 thousand visitors.

The cover was done by 4,446 professionals in local press, national, and international. The carnival was broadcast to 135 countries through 65 radio stations, 75 magazines, 139 producers of video, 97 newspapers (21 international), 14 tv stations, and 168 websites.[52]

Rei Momo: The King of Carnival, Momo, is handed the keys to the city in the morning, on the Thursday before Fat Tuesday, and the party officially begins. Camarotes: These grandstands line the street in the neighborhood of Campo Grande. Watch the show from here without being trampled by the crowd. Trios Eléctricos: Outfitted with deafening sound systems, these 60-foot-long trucks carry a kick line of gyrating, scantily clad dancers along with the city's best-loved performers, among them Ivete Sangalo, Daniela Mercury, Cláudia Leitte, Chiclete com Banana, Carlinhos Brown, and others.[53]

The music played during Carnaval includes Axé and Samba-reggae. Many "blocos" participate in Carnaval, the "blocos afros" like Malé Debalé, Olodum and Filhos de Gandhi being the most famous of them. Carnival is heavily policed. Stands with five or six seated police officers are erected everywhere and the streets are constantly patrolled by police groups moving in single file.

The Osmar Circuit: goes from Campo Grande to Castro Alves square, The Downtown Circuit, in Downtown and Pelourinho, and The Dodô Circuit; goes from Farol da Barra to Ondina, along the coast. The Osmar circuit is the oldest circuit. It is also where the event's most

Salvador's Street Carnival is the biggest in the world.

Campo Grande Circuit, on September Seven Avenue.

traditional groups parades. In Dodô, where the artist box seats are located, the party becomes lively toward the end of the afternoon and it continues until morning.

The three Carnival Circuits are:

- The Campo Grande - Praça Castro Alves Circuit, also called the "Osmar" Circuit, or simply the "Avenidas" ("Avenues");
- The Barra - Ondina Circuit, also called the "Dodô" Circuit;
- The Pelourinho Circuit, also called the "Batatinha" ("Little potato") Circuit.

Barra - Ondina Circuit, on Oceanic Avenue.

Summer Festival

The Salvador Summer Festival, is an annual five-day music extravaganza that this year is to feature its usual who's who of Brazilian popular music: Daniela Mercury, Eva, Capital Inicial, Titãs, Skank, Jota Quest, Ivete Sangalo, Chiclete com Banana, Ana Carolina, and others. The price of admission has yet to be set. Attractions international as Akon, Gloria Gaynor, Men at Work, Eagle-Eye Cherry, Fatboy Slim, Ben Harper, Manu Chao, Westlife, The Gladiators and Alanis Morissette already sang in Summer Festival.

Funk and Bahia Funk Dances

Funk has become a musical genre in Brazil that exemplifies how many influences, in and out of Brazil, merged with Brazilian culture in the 20th century to form a new hybrid sound.

Although funk was embraced by many parts of Brazil, its sound would eventually become localized so the music would differ from city to city. This difference can be viewed with the funk scenes in Rio de Janeiro and Salvador. The music and the environment are all representative of the city where one listens to funk music.

For instance, the music played in Salvador at a Black Bahia Funk Ball is more American than its counterpart in Rio de Janeiro. Music material from Rio, which sells reasonably well around Rio, is poorly known in Salvador and, in any case, held to be inferior and "less modern" than funk sung in English. Another difference can be seen with the funk dancehalls. The Ball incorporates the entire setting, which entails the attire, the slang, the specific way of dancing break, the decoration, the organization of permanent dance groups.[54]

Libraries

The first books that arrived in Salvador, were brought by the Jesuits, who came with Tomé de Souza.[55] The first libraries or bookstores that appeared were under the control of the religious missionaries and were mostly composed of books on religion. Areas combining leisure and culture, Salvador's libraries are an entertainment option for tourists and researchers. Some of these spaces have religious origins, some of them are temples of knowledge accessible only to a few, due to the fragility of the relics they contain.

The *Gabinete Português de Leitura*

The Benedictine, Carmelites, Franciscans and Capuchin orders have in Salvador, titles related to fundamental aspects of the state's history, being important for a comprehensive view of the political, religious, moral and artistic formation of the city. Conversely to the restrictive religious libraries, the public libraries and the ones linked to institutions that give incentive to culture and information, provide the general public with a variety of titles.

Handcraft

Local culture.

The handcraft legacy of Bahia using only raw materials (straw, leather, clay, wood, seashells and beads), the most rudimentary crafts are reasonably inexpensive. Other pieces are created with the use of metals like gold, silver, copper and brass. The most sophisticated ones are ornamented with precious and semi-precious gems. The craftsmen and women generally choose religion as the main theme of their work.

They portray the images of Catholic saints and Candomble deities on their pieces. The good luck charms such as the clenched fist, the four-leaf clover, the garlic and the famous Bonfim ribbons express the city's religious syncretism. Nature is also portrayed on these pieces, reflecting the local wildlife. Music appears in the atabaque drums, the rain sticks, the water drums and the famous berimbau, along with other typical instruments.[56]

Salvador holds an international reputation as a city where musical instruments that produce unique sounds are made. These instruments are frequently used by world-famous artists in their recording sessions. A place to see Salvador's handcrafts production is Mercado Modelo, which is the biggest handcraft center in Latin America.[57] Pieces can also be purchased at Instituto de Artesanato de Mauá and at Instituto do Patrimônio Artístico e Cultural (IPAC). These are organizations that promote typical art in Bahia.

Transportation

International Airport

Deputado Luís Eduardo Magalhães International Airport is located in an area of more than 10 million square meters between sand dunes and native vegetation(The Biggest of North/Northeast). The airport lies 40 km (25 mi) north of Downtown Salvador and the road to the airport has already become one of the city's main scenic attractions. In 2011, the airport handled 6,948,020 passengers and 114,946 aircraft movements,[58] placing it 7th busiest airport in Brazil in terms of passengers. The airport's use has been growing at an average of 14% a year and now is responsible for more than 30% of passenger movement in Northeastern Brazil.

Deputado Luís Eduardo Magalhães International Airport (SSA).

Port

One marina of the city.

With cargo volume that grows year after year following the same economic development rhythm implemented in the State, the Port of Salvador, located in the Bahia de Todos os Santos, holds status as the port with the highest movement of containers of the North/Northeast and the second-leading fruit exporter in Brazil. The port's facilities operate from 8:00 AM to 12:00 PM and from 1:30 PM to 5:30 PM.

The ability to handle high shipping volume has positioned the port of Salvador for new investments in technological modernization, and the port is noted for implementing a high level of operational flexibility and competitive rates. The goal of port officials is to offer the necessary infrastructure for the movement of goods, while simultaneously meeting the needs of international importers and exporters.

Metro

Salvador Metro System is under construction, and its 1st phase will be ready in March 2008, between Lapa and Acceso Norte Stations, and in 2009 will be ready the stations between Acceso Norte and Pirajá. In 2009 it will have 12.5 km (7.8 mi) and 8 stations and will have link with the bus system.

View of Salvador Metro.

The main shareholders in Metro Salvador are the Spanish companies Construcciones y Auxiliar de Ferrocarriles, Dimetronic, and ICF. It is expected that Metro Salvador will invest US$ 150 million in rolling stock and signalling and telecommunications equipment. The contract covers the first 11.9 km (7.4 mi) line from Pirajá to Lapa, which is due to open in 2003. The project is also financed by a US$ 150 million World Bank loan and contributions from the federal, Bahia state, and Salvador city governments.[59]

Salvador Metro system is one of the actions of urban mobility that will be deployed until the 2014 FIFA World Cup. The connection of Line 2 with Line 1 of Salvador Metro contributes to connect the International Airport to Downtown Salvador and the Fonte Nova Stadium. The new Line 2 of Salvador Metro integrates the metro stations of the Rótula do Abacaxi and the beach city of Lauro de Freitas in the metropolitan area, passing through the Salvador International Airport, with the Airport metro station.[60]

Highways

Green Line Highway.

The BR-101 and BR-116 federal highways cross Bahia from north to south, connecting Salvador to the rest of the country. At the Feira de Santana junction, take the BR-324 state highway. The capital of Bahia is served by several coach companies from almost every Brazilian state. BR-242, starting at São Roque do Paraguaçu (transversal direction), is linked to BR-116, bound to the middle–west region. Among the state highways stands BA-099, which makes connection to the north coast and BA-001, which makes connection to the south of Bahia. Buses provide direct service to most major Brazilian cities, including Rio de Janeiro, São Paulo, and Brasília, as well as regional destinations. In 2007, the city had 586,951 vehicles, the largest number of the Northern and Northeastern Brazil.[61]

Four paved highways connect the city to the national highway system. Running north from the Farol (lighthouse) de Itapoã are hundreds of miles of wonderful beaches. These beaches are accessible via the BA-099 Highway or (Line of Coconut and Green Line), a (toll) road, kept in excellent condition, running parallel to the coast, with access roads leading off to the coast itself. The road runs along dunes of snow-white sand, and the coast itself is an almost unbroken line of coconut palms. The communities along this coast range from fishing villages to Praia do Forte.

Neighborhoods

Barra Neighborhood in South Zone.

Although the creation of Salvador was masterminded by the Kingdom of Portugal and its project conducted by the Portuguese engineer Luís Dias (who was responsible for the city's original design), the continuous growth of the capital through the decades was completely spontaneous. The walls of the city-fortress could not hold the expansion of the city, towards the Carmo and the area where now stands Castro Alves Square. At the time of its foundation, Salvador had only two squares and the first neighborhood ever built here was the Historic City Center. Pelourinho and Carmo came subsequently, created as a consequence of the growing need of space that the religious orders had. With the rapid expansion, the neighborhoods grew and many of them were clustered in the same area, so today there are not accurate records as to their exact number. For urban management purposes, the city is currently divided on 17 political-administrative zones. However, due to their very cultural relevance and to postal conveniences, the importance of the neighborhoods of Salvador remains intact. They represent the city's lively atmosphere and its cosmopolitan character.

Caminho das Árvores Neighborhood.

Salvador is divided into a number of distinct neighborhoods, with the most well known districts being Pelourinho, the Historic Centre, Comércio, and Downtown, all located in West Zone. Barra, with its Farol da Barra, beaches and which is where one of the Carnival circuits begins, Barra is home of the Portuguese Hospital and Spanish Hospital, the neighborhood is located in South Zone. Vitória, a neighborhood with many high rise buildings, is located in South Zone. Campo Grande, with its Dois de Julho Square and the monument to Bahia's independence, is also located in South Zone, as is Graça, an important residential area. Ondina, with Salvador's Zoobotanical Garden and the site where the Barra-Ondina Carnival circuit ends, the neighborhood is home of the Spanish Club, is also a neighborhood in the South Zone.

Itaigara, Pituba, Horto Florestal, Caminho das Árvores, Loteamento Aquárius, Brotas, Stiep, Costa Azul, Armação, Jaguaribe and Stella Maris are the wealthiest neighborhoods in the East Zone and the city. Rio Vermelho, a neighborhood with a rich architectural history and numerous restaurants and bars, is located in the South Zone. Itapoã, known throughout Brazil as the home of Vinicius de Moraes and for being the setting of the song "Tarde em Itapoã", is located in East Zone.

The Northwest area of the city in along the Bay of All Saints, also known as *Cidade Baixa* ("Lower city"), contains the impoverished suburban neighborhoods of Periperi, Paripe, Lobato, Liberdade, Nova Esperança, and Calçada. The neighborhood of Liberdade (Liberty) has the largest proportion of Afro-Brazilians of Salvador and Brazil.[62]

Sports

Salvador provides visitors and residents with various sport activities. The Fonte Nova Stadium, also known as Estádio Octávio Mangabeira is a football stadium inaugurated on January 28, 1951 in Salvador, Bahia, with a maximum capacity of 66,080 people. The stadium is owned by the Bahia government, and is the home ground of Esporte Clube Bahia. Its formal name honors Octávio Cavalcanti Mangabeira, a civil engineer, journalist, and former Bahia state governor from 1947 to 1954. The stadium is nicknamed Fonte Nova, because it is located at Ladeira das Fontes das Pedras. The stadium was in 2007 closed due to an accident, and the E.C. Bahia home matches now happen in another stadium, in Pituaçu.

Colorful houses in the Surfing area of Barra.

Esporte Clube Bahia and Esporte Clube Vitória are Salvador's main football teams. Bahia has won 2 national titles, Brazil Trophy in 1959 and the Brazilian League in 1988, while Vitória was a runner up in the Brazilian league in 1993 and Brazil Cup in 2010.

Salvador has two large green areas for the practice of golf. Cajazeiras Golf and Country Club has a 18-hole course, instructors, caddies and equipment for rent. Itapuã Golf club, located in the area of the Sofitel Hotel, has a 9-hole course, equipment store, caddies and clubs for rent. Tennis is very popular among Salvador's elites, with a great number of players and tournaments in the city's private clubs. Brasil Open, the country's most important tournament happens every year in Bahia.

Manoel Barradas Stadium.

During the last decades, volleyball has grown steadily in Salvador, especially after the gold medal won by Brazil in the 1992 Summer Olympics in Barcelona. The most important tournaments in Bahia are the State Championship, the State League tournament and the Primavera Games, and the main teams are Associação Atlética da Bahia, Bahiano de Tênis, and Clube the Regatas Itapagipe. There are also beach volleyball events. Salvador has housed many international tournaments. Federação Bahira de Voleibol (the state league) can inform the schedule of tournaments. Bowling is practiced both by teenagers and adults in Salvador. Boliche do Aeroclube and Space Bowling are equipped with automatic lanes as well as a complete bar infrastructure.

Bahia's basketball league exists since 1993 and has 57 teams. The sport is very popular in the city of Salvador, especially among students.[63] There are several courts scattered across the city, where is possible to play for free, like the one located at Bahia Sol square, where people play.[64] There are also several gymnasiums, in clubs like Bahiano de Tênis and Associação Atlética and the Antonio Balbino Gymnasiums (popularly known as "Balbininho"), which is an arena that can hold up to 7,000 people.

Arena Fonte Nova, the stadium of the 2014 FIFA World Cup.

Todos os Santos Bay and Salvador's climatic conditions are ideal for competition and recreational sailing. The city is equipped with good infrastructure for practice of sailing, such as rental and sale of dock space, boat maintenance, restaurants, snack bar, convenience stores, nautical products stores, boat rental agencies, VHF and SSB communication systems, events, and total assistance to crews. The large number of sailing events organized by clubs and syndicates, like oceanic races and typical boats (wooden fishing boats and canoes) races, demonstrates the sport's growing force. Currently, Salvador has a national racing schedule with dozens of events, also receiving the Mini Transat 6.50 and Les Illes du Soleil races.

Rowing boat races started in the city more than a hundred years ago.[65] It was originally practiced by young men from traditional families, who spent their summer vacations there. The sport is a leisure option in Cidade Baixa (the lower part of the city). Esporte Clube Vitória and Clube São Salvador were the pioneers in the sport. Nowadays, these two entities and also Clube de Regatas Itapagipe lead the competitions that take place in the city. With the recent renovation of the Dique do Tororó area, Salvador received new lanes for the practice of the sport.

Notable residents

- Acelino Freitas, boxer.
- Adriana Lima, supermodel
- Antônio Carlos Magalhães, politician.
- Antônio Carlos Vovô, leader of Ilê Aiyê Afro Bloco.
- Antônio Rodrigo Nogueira, (Minotauro), MMA fighter.
- Bebeto Gama, football forward.
- Caetano Veloso, musician.
- Carlinhos Brown, singer.
- Castro Alves, poet.
- Cláudia Leitte, singer.
- Daniela Mercury, musician.
- Dias Gomes, playwright.
- Dorival Caymmi, singer.
- Edvaldo Valério, swimmer.
- Gal Costa, singer.
- Gilberto Gil, singer.
- Glauber Rocha, movie director.
- Gregório de Mattos, poet.
- Irmã Dulce, Catholic nun.
- Itamar Franco, politician.
- Ivete Sangalo, singer.
- João Gilberto, musician.

Supermodel Adriana Lima (left) is from Salvador.

- João Ubaldo Ribeiro, writer.
- Jorge Amado, writer.
- Junior Dos Santos, mixed martial artist.
- Lateef Crowder Dos Santos, Capoeira practitioner
- Lázaro Ramos, actor.
- Lyoto Machida, mixed martial artist.
- Manuel dos Reis Machado (Bimba), capoeira master.
- Marcos Andre Batista Santos (Vampeta), soccer player.
- Margareth Menezes, singer.
- Maria Bethânia, singer.
- Milton Santos, geograph.
- Nelson de Jesus Silva (Dida), soccer goalkeeper.
- Pitty, musician.
- Raul Seixas, musician.
- Ricardo Santos, beach volleyball player.
- Ruy Barbosa de Oliveira, writer, jurist and politician.
- Saulo Fernandes, singer.
- Simone Bittencourt, singer.
- Tom Zé, musician.
- Tony Kanaan, race car driver.
- Wagner Moura, actor.
- Vicente Ferreira Pastinha, capoeira master

Sister cities

Salvador's sister cities are:[66]

Country	City	State / Region	Since
United States	Los Angeles	California	1962[66]
Portugal	Lisbon	Lisboa Region	1985[66]
Portugal	Angra do Heroísmo	Azores	1985[66]
Portugal	Cascais	Lisbon Region	1985[66]
Benin	Cotonou	Littoral Department	1987[66]
Spain	Pontevedra	Galicia	1992[66]
Cuba	Havana	La Havana	1993[66]
Italy	Sciacca	Sicily	2001[66]
China	Harbin	Heilongjiang	2003[66]
United States	Miami	Florida	2006[67]

References

[1] http://www.salvador.ba.gov.br/
[2] Brickell, Margaret (July 1991). "If You Only Have a Day in Salvador da Bahia" (http://books.google.com.au/books?id=ey0DAAAAMBAJ&pg=PA25&dq=sao+salvador+holy+savior+bahia&hl=en&ei=LF26TamNG9OE0QHS7tTIBQ&sa=X&oi=book_result&ct=result&resnum=1&ved=0CEsQ6AEwAA#v=onepage&q=sao salvador holy savior bahia&f=false). *Cruise Travel* **13** (1): 25–26. . Retrieved 29 April 2011.
[3] Graham, Sandra Lauderdale (2002). *Caetana says no: women's stories from a Brazilian slave society*. Cambridge: Cambridge University Press. pp. 3. ISBN 0-521-89353-4.
[4] (PDF) *Geography* (http://www.alovelyworld.com/webbresil/htmgb/bre012.htm). Salvador, Brazil: Aloveworld. 2006. ISBN 85-240-3919-1. . Retrieved 2007-07-18.
[5] (http://www.climatefinder.com/places/SBSV)
[6] (http://isbor2011.com/conteudo/show/id/11)
[7] (http://www.ridim-br.mus.ufba.br/ridim2011/en/history.html)
[8] http://en.wikipedia.org/wiki/Kahal_Zur_Israel_Synagogue|The
[9] (http://eyesonbrazil.com/2008/07/15/salvador-da-bahia-first-national-capital/)
[10] (http://www.hmdb.org/marker.asp?marker=26125)
[11] (http://www.ywamcity.org/city.asp?id=75)
[12] "Weatherbase: Historical Weather for Salvador" (http://www.weatherbase.com/weather/weather.php3?s=84238&refer=&units=metric). July 2011. .
[13] 2010 IGBE Census (**Portuguese**)[[Category:Articles with Portuguese language external links (http://www.censo2010.ibge.gov.br/dados_divulgados/index.php?uf=29)]]
[14] 2010 IGBE Census (**Portuguese**)[[Category:Articles with Portuguese language external links (http://www.censo2010.ibge.gov.br/painel/?nivel=mn)]]
[15] The largest Brazilian cities - 2010 IBGE Census (http://noticias.uol.com.br/cotidiano/2010/11/04/maiores-cidades-do-brasil-crescem-menos-do-que-resto-do-pais-aponta-censo.jhtm)
[16] By FROMMER'S (2006-11-20). "Introduction to Bahia - New York Times" (http://travel.nytimes.com/frommers/travel/guides/central-and-south-america/brazil/bahia/frm_bahia_2852010001.html). Travel.nytimes.com. . Retrieved 2010-04-17.
[17] http://web2.sbg.org.br/congress/sbg2008/pdfs2008/23959.pdf
[18] "Barsa Planeta Ltda" (http://brasil.planetasaber.com/default.asp). Brasil.planetasaber. . Retrieved 2010-04-17.
[19] "Religion in Salvador by IBGE" (http://www.sim.salvador.ba.gov.br/indicadores/index.php). Sim.salvador.ba.gov.br. . Retrieved 2010-04-17.
[20] About Salvador (http://www.worldpeacejournal.com/apps/blog/show/prev?from_id=7196252&sms_ss=twitter&at_xt=4de040cf9da5b2dc,0)
[21] "Salvador - Great Cities (U.S. Website)" (http://www.greatcities.org/pg.asp?ID=34). Great Cities. . Retrieved 2010-04-17.
[22] (http://www.topdobrasil.com.br/praias/nordeste/ba/praias-de-salvador.php)
[23] Gerador Automático de Meta-Tags <http://buscas.com.br/meta-tags>. "Historic Churches in Pelourinho" (http://www.visiteabahia.com.br/visite/salvador/pelourinho/index.php). Visiteabahia.com.br. . Retrieved 2010-04-17.
[24] "Folha Online - Growth in construction has attracted many international investors" (http://www1.folha.uol.com.br/folha/bbc/ult272u59941.shtml). .folha.uol.com.br. 1970-01-01. . Retrieved 2010-04-17.
[25] "Car Models - Ford Bahia" (http://www.parana-online.com.br/editoria/economia/news/410985/?noticia=FORD+AMPLIARA+FABRICA+DE+CAMACARI+NA+BAHIA). Parana-online.com.br. . Retrieved 2010-04-17.
[26] Ford Motor Company in Salvador Metropolitan Area (**Portuguese**)[[Category:Articles with Portuguese language external links (http://www.terra.com.br/istoedinheiro/428/negocios/fabrica_ford.htm)]]
[27] Jac Motors in Bahia (**Portuguese**)[[Category:Articles with Portuguese language external links (http://g1.globo.com/videos/bahia/v/jac-motors-anuncia-instalacao-da-fabrica-de-automoveis-no-polo-industrial-de-camacari/1699006/)]]
[28] Monsanto Company in Salvador (**Portuguese**)[[Category:Articles with Portuguese language external links (http://www.pautasocial.com.br/pauta.asp?idPauta=37175)]]
[29] 2010 IBGE Census (**Portuguese**)[[Category:Articles with Portuguese language external links (http://georgelins.com/2010/12/12/pib-as-100-maiores-cidades-do-brasil-ibge-2010/)]]
[30] Tourism in Salvador (**English**) (http://traveleye.com/travel_guide/cit/760/Salvador.html)
[31] Gavin McOwan (2007-02-16). "Top 10 beaches of the world | Travel" (http://www.guardian.co.uk/travel/2007/feb/16/beach.top10?page=2). London: guardian.co.uk. . Retrieved 2010-04-17.
[32] Salvador Guide Information (**English**) (http://www.drhostel.com/travelguide/salvador-tourist-guide-information/)
[33] http://www.escolapanamericana.com/faq.htm
[34] http://www.uneb.br
[35] http://www.unifacs.br
[36] http://www.ftc.br/
[37] http://www.cefetba.br

[38] http://www.frb.br
[39] http://www.castroalves.br
[40] http://www.jorgeamado.edu.br/Default.html
[41] http://www.bahiana.edu.br/
[42] "Top High schools of Salvador" (http://veja.abril.com.br/melhor_da_cidade/salvador/ensino.shtml). Veja.abril.com.br. . Retrieved 2010-04-17.
[43] http://whc.unesco.org/en/list/309
[44] http://whc.unesco.org/en/list
[45] http://whc.unesco.org/en/list/?search=&search_by_country=&type=&media=&region=&order=region
[46] Projecto Brazil (**English**) (http://projectobrazil.blogspot.com/2008/07/salvador-de-bahia-information.html)
[47] "New Pelourinho" (http://gosouthamerica.about.com/cs/southamerica/a/BraPelourinho.htm). Gosouthamerica.about.com. 2010-03-05. . Retrieved 2010-04-17.
[48] Brazil, Projecto (2008-07-25). "Portuguese language in the Baroque era" (http://projectobrazil.blogspot.com/2008/07/salvador-de-bahia-information.html). Projectobrazil.blogspot.com. . Retrieved 2010-04-17.
[49] Caopeira (**English**) (http://www.travelblog.org/South-America/Brazil/Bahia/Salvador/blog-618906.html)
[50] "Capoeira Information" (http://www.brazilplaces.com/capoeira-brazil.html). Brazilplaces.com. . Retrieved 2010-04-17.
[51] "Carnaval of Salvador" (http://home.centraldocarnaval.com.br/primeiro_carnaval.asp). Home.centraldocarnaval.com.br. . Retrieved 2010-04-17.
[52] "Numbers of Carnival - Salvador" (http://translate.google.com/translate?u=www.visiteabahia.com.br/visite/carnaval/suahistoria/ultimos.php&langpair=pt). Translate.google.com. . Retrieved 2010-04-17.
[53] Brooke, James (1993-02-14). "Carnival of Salvador in The" (http://query.nytimes.com/gst/fullpage.html?res=9F0CE5DB143BF937A25751C0A965958260). New York Times. . Retrieved 2010-04-17.
[54] Osmundo Pinho. "Ethnographies of the Brau: body, masculinity and race in the reafricanization in Salvador." In Estudos Feministas. 2006. University of Campinas
[55] "Tomé de Souza in Salvador" (http://muse.jhu.edu/login?uri=/journals/the_americas/v061/61.3metcalf.html). Muse.jhu.edu. . Retrieved 2010-04-17.
[56] Salvador Information (**English**) (http://www.salvadorhotels.brazilhotels.4k.com/Culture-salvador.php)
[57] "Model Market of Salvador" (http://www.portalmercadomodelo.com.br/). Portalmercadomodelo.com.br. . Retrieved 2010-04-17.
[58] "Airport statistics for 2011 (Infraero) - Deputado Luís Eduardo Magalhães International Airport" (http://www.infraero.gov.br/images/stories/Estatistica/2011/Outubro.pdf) (PDF). . Retrieved 2011.
[59] "Salvador Metro" (http://findarticles.com/p/articles/mi_m0BQQ/is_9_41/ai_80931933/). Findarticles.com. 2001. . Retrieved 2010-04-17.
[60] 2014 FIFA World Cup (**Portuguese**)[[Category:Articles with Portuguese language external links (http://www.portal2014.org.br/noticias/8482/METRO+DEVE+CHEGAR+A+SALVADOR+ANTES+DA+COPA.html)]]
[61] "Salvador City Hall - Number of Vehicles" (http://www.sim.salvador.ba.gov.br/indicadores/index.php). Sim.salvador.ba.gov.br. . Retrieved 2010-04-17.
[62] "Liberdade Neighborhood" (http://www.smec.salvador.ba.gov.br/net/piraja/liberdad.htm). Smec.salvador.ba.gov.br. . Retrieved 2010-04-17.
[63] "Basketball in Salvador" (http://www.asbacsalvador.com.br/basquete.htm). Asbacsalvador.com.br. . Retrieved 2010-04-17.
[64] "Brazilian Federation of Basketball" (http://www.digidata.com.br/fbbm/clip.php?consulta=sim&atual=Clipping&codcli=587). Digidata.com.br. . Retrieved 2010-04-17.
[65] "Rowing boat in Salvador" (http://www.campos.rj.gov.br/noticia.php?id=15339). Campos.rj.gov.br. . Retrieved 2010-04-17.
[66] "Mayor's International Council Sister Cities Program" (http://www.secri.salvador.ba.gov.br/index.php?option=com_content&task=view&id=40&Itemid=47). Salvador, Bahia. . Retrieved 2008-08-17.
[67] Miami and Salvador are Sister Cities (http://www.miamihotels.usahotels.4k.com/Sister-cities-miami.phpp)

External links

- Pelourinho of Salvador, Bahia Digital Media Archive (http://archive.cyark.org/salvador-da-bahia-intro) (creative commons-licensed photos, laser scans, panoramas), data from a Federal University of Bahia/University of Ferrara/Leica Geosystems/CyArk research partnership

Official

- **(Portuguese)** City website (http://www.salvador.ba.gov.br/)
- City Tourism Portal (http://www.salvadordabahia.ba.gov.br/index_anim.asp?idLinguagem=2)
- Salvador Bahia (http://www.salvadorbahiaguide.com/)

Campeonato_Baiano

Countries	Brazil
Confederation	CBF
	Federação Bahiana de Futebol
Founded	1905
Number of teams	12
Domestic cup(s)	Copa do Brasil
Current champions	Bahia de Feira (2011)
Most championships	Bahia (43 titles)
Website	www.fbf.org.br [1]

2012 Campeonato Baiano

The **Campeonato Baiano** is the football league of the state of Bahia, Brazil. The championship has been played since 1905 without interruption.

2008 format

First stage:

The 12 teams play in double round-robin in 22 rounds. The top 4 qualify for the Final Stage, the bottom team is relegated.

Final stage:

The 4 teams play in double round-robin in 6 rounds. The winners of Final Stage is the champions. The top 3 teams (except the clubs of Série A, Série B and Série C) qualify for the Série D.

Clubs

First Division 2007

- **Alagoinhas** Atlético Clube
- Esporte Clube **Bahia**
- **Camaçari** Futebol Clube
- **Catuense** Futebol S/A
- **Colo-Colo** de Ilhéus Futebol e Regatas
- **Fluminense** de Feira Futebol Clube
- Esporte Clube **Ipitanga** da Bahia Ltda
- **Itabuna** Esporte Clube
- **Juazeiro** Social Clube
- Esporte Clube **Poções**
- Esporte Clube Primeiro Passo de **Vitória da Conquista**
- Esporte Clube **Vitória**

Second Division 2007

- Associação Desportiva Comunitária **Astro**
- Sport Clube **Camaçariense**

- **Conquista** Futebol Clube
- **Feirense** Esporte Clube
- **Galícia** Esporte Clube
- **Guanambi** Atlético Clube
- Associação Desportiva **Leônico**

Not enter in Second Division 2007

- **Barreiras** Esporte Clube
- **Cruzeiro** Futebol Clube
- Sport Club **Jacuipense**
- **Real Salvador** Esporte Clube Ltda.
- **Serrano** Sport Club
- **Serrinha** Esporte Clube
- Esporte Clube **Ypiranga**

Champions

Year	Champions
1905	Clube Internacional de Cricket (Salvador)
1906	São Salvador (Salvador)
1907	São Salvador (Salvador)
1908	Vitória (Salvador)
1909	Vitória (Salvador)
1910	Sport Club Santos Dumont (Salvador)
1911	Sport Club Bahia (Salvador)
1912	Atlético Futebol Clube (Salvador)
1913	Fluminense (Salvador)
1914	S. C. Internacional (Salvador)
1915	Fluminense (Salvador)
1916	Sport Club República (Salvador)
1917	Ypiranga (Salvador)
1918	Ypiranga (Salvador)
1919	Botafogo (Salvador)
1920	Ypiranga (Salvador)
1921	Ypiranga (Salvador)
1922	Botafogo (Salvador)
1923	Botafogo (Salvador)
1924	Associação Atlética da Bahia (Salvador)
1925	Ypiranga (Salvador)
1926	Botafogo (Salvador)
1927	Clube Bahiano de Tênis (Salvador)
1928	Ypiranga (Salvador)
1929	Ypiranga (Salvador)

1930	Botafogo (Salvador)
1931	Bahia (Salvador)
1932	Ypiranga (Salvador)
1933	Bahia (Salvador)
1934	Bahia (Salvador)
1935	Botafogo (Salvador)
1936	Bahia (Salvador)
1937	Galícia (Salvador)
1938	Bahia (Salvador) and Botafogo (Salvador)
1939	Ypiranga (Salvador)
1940	Bahia (Salvador)
1941	Galícia (Salvador)
1942	Galícia (Salvador)
1943	Galícia (Salvador)
1944	Bahia (Salvador)
1945	Bahia (Salvador)
1946	Guarany (Salvador)
1947	Bahia (Salvador)
1948	Bahia (Salvador)
1949	Bahia (Salvador)
1950	Bahia (Salvador)
1951	Ypiranga (Salvador)
1952	Bahia (Salvador)
1953	Vitória (Salvador)
1954	Bahia (Salvador)
1955	Vitória (Salvador)
1956	Bahia (Salvador)
1957	Vitória (Salvador)
1958	Bahia (Salvador)
1959	Bahia (Salvador)
1960	Bahia (Salvador)
1961	Bahia (Salvador)
1962	Bahia (Salvador)
1963	Fluminense de Feira (Feira de Santana)
1964	Vitória (Salvador)
1965	Vitória (Salvador)
1966	Leônico (Salvador)
1967	Bahia (Salvador)
1968	Galícia (Salvador)

1969	Fluminense de Feira (Feira de Santana)
1970	Bahia (Salvador)
1971	Bahia (Salvador)
1972	Vitória (Salvador)
1973	Bahia (Salvador)
1974	Bahia (Salvador)
1975	Bahia (Salvador)
1976	Bahia (Salvador)
1977	Bahia (Salvador)
1978	Bahia (Salvador)
1979	Bahia (Salvador)
1980	Vitória (Salvador)
1981	Bahia (Salvador)
1982	Bahia (Salvador)
1983	Bahia (Salvador)
1984	Bahia (Salvador)
1985	Vitória (Salvador)
1986	Bahia (Salvador)
1987	Bahia (Salvador)
1988	Bahia (Salvador)
1989	Vitória (Salvador)
1990	Vitória (Salvador)
1991	Bahia (Salvador)
1992	Vitória (Salvador)
1993	Bahia (Salvador)
1994	Bahia (Salvador)
1995	Vitória (Salvador)
1996	Vitória (Salvador)
1997	Vitória (Salvador)
1998	Bahia (Salvador)
1999	Bahia (Salvador) and Vitória (Salvador)
2000	Vitória (Salvador)
2001	Bahia (Salvador)
2002	Palmeiras do Nordeste [1] (Feira de Santana) (Campeonato da Federação) and Vitória (Salvador) (Supercampeonato)
2003	Vitória (Salvador)
2004	Vitória (Salvador)
2005	Vitória (Salvador)
2006	Colo-Colo (Ilhéus)
2007	Vitória (Salvador)

2008	Vitória (Salvador)
2009	Vitória (Salvador)
2010	Vitória (Salvador)
2011	Bahia de Feira (Feira de Santana)

(1) Palmeiras do Nordeste is currently named Feirense.

Titles by team

Team	Winners	Runner-ups
Esporte Clube Bahia (Salvador)	43**	12
Esporte Clube Vitória (Salvador)	26*	12
Esporte Clube Ypiranga (Salvador)	10	10
Sport Club Botafogo (Salvador)	7*	7
Galícia Esporte Clube (Salvador)	5	9
Fluminense de Feira Futebol Clube (Feira de Santana)	2	6
Fluminense de Salvador (Salvador)	2	6
Clube de Natação e Regatas São Salvador (Salvador)	2	1
Associação Atlética da Bahia (Salvador)	2	4
Atlético Futebol Clube (Salvador)	1	0
Bahia de Feira (Feira de Santana)	1	0
Sport Club Bahia (Salvador)	1	0
Clube Internacional de Cricket (Salvador)	1	0
Associação Desportiva Guarany (Salvador)	1	0
Sport Club Internacional (Salvador)	1	0
Associação Desportiva Leônico (Salvador)	1	2
Sport Club República (Salvador)	1	0
Sport Club Santos Dumont (Salvador)	1	2
Clube Bahiano de Tênis (Salvador)	1	1
Feirense Esporte Clube (Feira de Santana)	1***	0
Colo Colo de Futebol e Regatas (Ilhéus)	1	0

(*) shared; (**) two titles shared; (***) Campeonato Baiano do Interior.

See also
- Campeonato Baiano (lower levels)

External links
- Federação Bahiana de Futebol - FBF Official Website [1]
- Globo Esporte - Campeonato Baiano 2008 [2]

References
[1] http://www.fbf.org.br
[2] http://globoesporte.globo.com/ESP/Home/0,,10067,00.html

Bahia

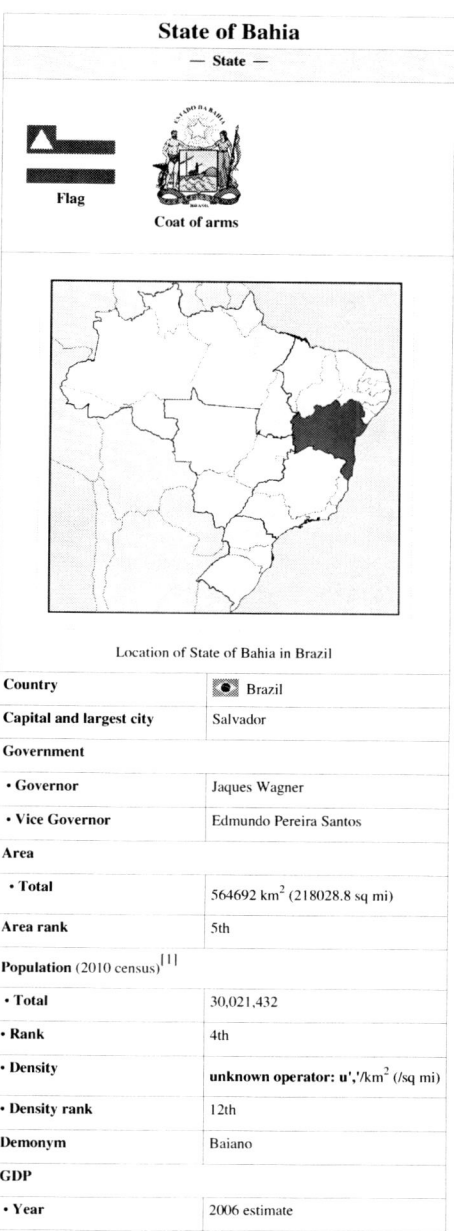

State of Bahia	
— State —	
Flag	Coat of arms
Location of State of Bahia in Brazil	
Country	Brazil
Capital and largest city	Salvador
Government	
• Governor	Jaques Wagner
• Vice Governor	Edmundo Pereira Santos
Area	
• Total	564692 km^2 (218028.8 sq mi)
Area rank	5th
Population (2010 census)[1]	
• Total	30,021,432
• Rank	4th
• Density	unknown operator: u','/km^2 (/sq mi)
• Density rank	12th
Demonym	Baiano
GDP	
• Year	2006 estimate

• Total	R$ 300,559,000,000 (6th)
• Per capita	R$ 40,922 (19th)
HDI	
• Year	2005
• Category	3.913 <very high>
Time zone	BRT (UTC-3)
• Summer (DST)	BRST (UTC-2)
Postal code	40000-000 to 48990-000
ISO 3166 code	BR-BA
Website	bahia.ba.gov.br [2]

Bahia (Portuguese pronunciation: [baˈi.ɐ])[3] is one of the 26 states of Brazil, and is located in the northeastern part of the country on the Atlantic coast. It is the fourth most populous Brazilian state after São Paulo, Minas Gerais and Rio de Janeiro, and the fifth-largest in size. Bahia's capital is the city of Salvador, or more properly, São Salvador da Bahia de Todos os Santos, and is located at the junction of the Atlantic Ocean and the Bay of All Saints, first seen by European sailors in 1501. The name "bahia" is an archaic spelling of the Portuguese word *baía*, meaning "bay".

Geography

The state's geographical regions comprise the Atlantic Forest. The *Recôncavo* region radiating from the Bay (the largest in Brazil), the site of sugar and tobacco cultivation. And the *Planalto*, which includes the fabled sertão region of Bahia's far interior. Bahia is bordered, in counterclockwise fashion, by Sergipe, Alagoas, Pernambuco and Piauí to the north, Goiás and Tocantins to the west, and Minas Gerais and Espírito Santo to the south. The State of Bahia is crossed from north to south by a mountain chain which is marked, in the map, as Chapada Diamantina. This same chain receives other names, like Serra do Espinhaço, in Minas Gerais, and Borborema, in Pernambuco and Paraíba.

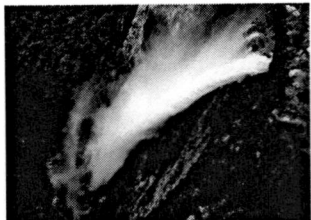

Fumaça Waterfall.

In some parts, the chain has the shape of "Chapadões", plateaus with abrupt edges, the most visited of such chapadões are in the National Park of Chapada Diamantina, in the middle of the State. The chain divides Bahia in two clearly distinct geographical zones. To the east, where once existed the exuberant Atlantic Forest, the soil is fertile and, despite high temperatures, rainy seasons are regular.

The predominant vegetation in the west is "cerrado". These tough conditions caused the interior to be much less developed than the coast. The state is also crossed by the river São Francisco, the most important of Brazilian northeast. São Francisco River is a permanent river, which continuously supplies water to this arid region when many other smaller rivers dry out. The São Francisco starts in Minas Gerais and goes on until the Atlantic, making borders between Bahia and Alagoas. There are short stretches of the river which are navigable, but mainly for cargoes. The large blue spot at the north is a huge dam built to hold water for the hydroelectric plant of Itaparica.

Climate

Tropical. In addition to its considerable size, it has the longest coastline of the country: 1,103 km long (685 miles; north coast: 143; Todos os Santos Bay: 124; and southern: 418). With 68% of its territory located in the semi-arid zone, the State presents diversified climates and an

Pratinha River.

average rainfall that varies from 363 to 2000 mm (14.3 to 79 in) per year, depending on the region. Regarding the weather, Bahia is one of the most privileged states of the country with the following temperatures: 19.2 to 26.6 °C (67 to 80 °F).

History

The Portuguese Pedro Álvares Cabral landed at what is now Porto Seguro City, on the southern coast of Bahia in 1500, and claimed the territory for Portugal. In 1549, Portugal established the city of Salvador, on a hill facing the Bay of All Saints. The city and surrounding captaincy served as the administrative and religious capital of Portugal's colonies in the Americas until 1763. The Dutch tried to hold control of Bahia but were defeated, only being able to seize Pernambuco. Charles Darwin visited Bahia in 1832 on his famous Voyage of The Beagle.

Historic Centre of Salvador.

The state was also the last area of Brazil to join the independent confederation. Some members in the elite remained loyal to the Portuguese crown after the rest of the country was granted independence. After several battles, mostly in Pirajá, the province was finally able to expel the Portuguese on July 2, 1823, known as Bahia Independence Day, a great popular celebration. In the state there is an ongoing discussion about the exact moment of Brazilian independence, because for almost all baianos, it really happened in Bahia with the battles, and not on September 7, when the Emperor, Pedro I, declared independence.

Bahia was a center of sugar cultivation from the 16th to the 18th centuries, and contains a number of historic towns, such as Cachoeira,

São Marcelo Fort, in the capital of the state.

dating from this era. Integral to the sugar economy was the importation of a vast number of African slaves; more than 37% of all slaves taken from Africa were sent to Brazil, mostly to be processed in Bahia before being sent to work in plantations elsewhere in the country. Bahia was also the site of one of the most important urban slave rebellions in the Americas in 1835, of particular note because it was one of the only predominantly Muslim slave revolts in the history of the New World. The oldest Roman Catholic cathedral and the first medical college in the country are located in Bahia's capital, which also has one of the highest percentage of churches of any state capital in Brazil. The Catholic Archbishop of São Salvador da Bahia, Geraldo Majella Agnelo, is the Cardinal Primate of Brazil.

Bahia Northeast Exploration

In 1620, the Bahia decided to set up colonies in other regions of northeastern of Brazil. The idea was given by the exitint Bahia West Islands Company, the state create three colonies: Vitória da Conquista(Pernambuco), São Vicente(Rio Grande do Norte) and Estrela da Santanna(Maranhão).

Demographics

According to the IBGE of 2008, there are 14,561,000 people residing in the state. The population density was 24.93 inhabitants per square kilometre (64.6 /sq mi).

Urbanization: 67.4% (2006); Population growth: 1.1% (1991–2000); Houses: 3,826,000 (2006).[4]

The last PNAD (National Research for Sample of Domiciles) census revealed the following numbers: 9,149,000 Brown (Multiracial) people (62.83%), 3,000,000 White people (20.60%), 2,328,000 Black people (15.99%), 42,000 Amerindian people (0.29%), 37,000 Asian people (0.26%).[5]

People in Bonfim Church. Religion in Bahia is a syncretic mix of European Catholicism and African religions.

View of Jequié.

City	Population
Salvador (the capital)	5,001,625
Feira de Santana	2,571,997
Vitória da Conquista	1,313,898
Juazeiro	1,230,538
Ilhéus	990,144
Itabuna	940,604
Jequié	805,964
Lauro de Freitas	444,492

Economy

The industrial sector is the largest component of GDP at 48.5%, followed by the service sector at 40.8%. Agriculture represents 10.7% of GDP (2004). Bahia exports: chemicals 22.4%, fuel 17.5%, mineral metallics 13%, paper 9.4%, cacao 5.6%, vehicles 4.8%, soybean 4.5% (2002).

Share of the Brazilian economy: 4.9% (2004).[6]

The state has the biggest GDP of the states of the North/Northeast. Bahia is the main producer and exporter of cacao in Brazil. In addition to important agricultural and industrial sectors, the state also has considerable mineral and petroleum deposits. In recent years, soy cultivation has increased substantially in the state. Bahia is the sixth largest economy in the country. In the mid 1950s, the Bahian economy could be considered a typical example of the primary-exporting model, which followed the subsistence production. For ten years, this dynamic was led by the cocoa crop, that used to be the state's main product and its most important source of income.

With the acceleration of the industrialization process in the 1970s, which started in the 1950s, the productive structure began to change. This process, which was not limited to the regional market, was inserted in the Brazilian industry matrix through the chemical (specially petrochemical) and metallurgical segment. Consequently, for the last twenty years, the dynamism of the Bahian economy has surpassed the rational economy, yielding higher growth rates than those achieved by the national economy. The industrial sector is expected to continue to be the main contributor to this growth, particularly from 1999 on, when the investments that are being made now in the chemical, petrochemical and automotive segment, and in agroindustry and food production will be consolidated.

The Bahian economy began 2005 in a very healthy state, with an exceptional trajectory of growth, once again presenting activity indicators superior to those of the Brazilian economy. Those numbers are the result of the endeavours of the Bahian Government, the result of increasing productive investment, and therefore, potential production, something that has been carried out through attractive enterprise policies in all segments of the economy, placing Bahia in a privileged position in the regional and national scenario. Today, the State has a differentiated economic profile. Bahian industry has continued to diversify and widen its productive base, with the implantation of new industrial segments, like the automobile and tyre industries, footwear and textiles, furniture, food and beverages, cosmetics and perfumes, information technology and naval development.

Itaparica Island.

Exceptional results can be seen in agriculture, commerce and tourism, where Bahia appears as one of the principal national destinations. For this to happen, the strategic position model of Bahia in the international tourism route was fundamental, with direct and regular flights to Europe, the United States, and the Southern Cone, due to the complementary governmental and private initiatives, besides the development of new tourist poles integrated to the local culture.

Chemical and Petrochemical

Bahia's Petrochemical Pole is the largest integrated complex in the Southern Hemisphere, and is the result of R$10 billion in investments, accounting for a third of the state's exports and for nearly half of the industrial production value.

Mining

Bahia is one of the richest states in minerals in the country, ranking third in Brazilian mineral production. The State's main products are gold, copper concentrate, magnesite, chromite, rock salt, barite, manganese, ornamental rocks, precious stones, talcum, phosphates and uranium.

Hydroelectric power plant in Sobradinho.

Automotive

In Bahia, the automotive sector has gained prominence since the creation of the Northeast Ford Complex in Camaçari (2001), and has become one of the most promising sectors of the Bahian economy. This enterprise, which was developed with the aim of generating 5,000 direct jobs and 55,000 indirect ones in 2005 has surpassed those expectations by creating 8,500 direct job positions and 85,000 indirect ones since its development.

Nowadays, Bahia produces about 10% of all vehicles produced in Brazil, occupying the third position in the national rankings. The Bahian automotive sector, led by Ford was in 2005 the third largest contributor (14.6%) to the Bahian GDP. It is important to highlight that Bahia had a 4.8% overall increase in its GDP, double the national performance, according to the Superintendency of Economic and Social Studies of Bahia (SEI)/Secretariat of Planning and IBGE.

Other market segments

Agribusiness; Footwear; Call Centers; Informatics, Electronics, and Telecommunications; Nautical; Paper and Pulp; Textiles; Plastic Transformation; and Tourism.

Tourism: Bahia's long coastline, beautiful beaches and cultural treasures make it one of Brazil's chief tourist destinations. In addition to the island of Itaparica, the town of Morro de São Paulo across the Bay on the northernmost tip of the southern coastline, and the large number of beaches between Ilhéus and Porto Seguro, on the southeastern coast, the littoral area north of Salvador, stretching towards the border with Sergipe, has become an important tourist destination. The *Costa do Sauípe* contains one of the largest resort hotel developments in Brazil and South America.

Airport of Ilhéus.

Regions of Bahia

The Coconut Coast

The Coconut Coast, in the northern of Bahia, corresponds to a total of 193 km (120 mi) of coastline, where coconut groves, dunes, rivers, swamps and sweet water lagoons are a constant scenario as well as the presence of the Atlantic Rain Forest. The Green Road, a road that connects Mangue Seco in the far north to Praia do Forte, crosses this beautiful region maintaining a critical distance from the areas of environmental preservation. For this reason the route is sometimes more than 10 km (6.2 mi) from the beach. At Praia do Forte, the road meets the Coconut Road]

(Estrada do Côco) and leads to Salvador, passing through spots, which are now integrated in the urban development of the state capital. In this region is located the Deputado Luís Eduardo Magalhães International Airport.

All Saints Bay

The largest bay on the Brazilian coast, Todos os Santos has a large number of islands with tropical beaches and vegetation. In its 1,052 square km, it contains 56 islands, receives sweet water from numerous rivers and creeks (especially the Paraguaçú and Subaé) and bathes the first capital of Brazil and the largest in the Northeast, Salvador, and more than ten municipalities. It is the largest navigable bay in Brazil and one of the most favorite spots for nautical sports, due to its regular breezes, medium annual temperature of 26 °C (79 °F) and sheltered waters. Todos os Santos Bay offers various leisure options, with hundreds of vessels of all different types, especially saveiros, schooners, motor boats, jet ski that criss-cross its crystalline waters on maritime excursions to the islands, and boat races. Major popular events and sport activities occur throughout the year, beginning on January 1, with the Procession of Bom Jesus dos Navegantes greeting the New Year.

View of Salvador.

Todos os Santos Bay has also been traditionally the venue for rowing contests at the Enseada dos Tainheiros, in Salvador and now the bay is included in the routes of the great international regattas, such as the Ralley Les Iles du Soleil, regatta Hong Kong Challenge and the Expo 98 Round the World Rally, which consider the bay an important stop along the route. The islands of the bay are a separate attraction. Some are privately owned, others were declared a state heritage and transformed into Environmental Protection Areas or ecological stations. Other islands are the patrimony of 12 municipalities located around the bay. Only a few are uninhabited and many have small communities where the natives live on fishing and tourism. All have common characteristics, such a calm sea, dense vegetation, especially coconuts and bananas, as well as vestiges of the Atlantic Forest. Of the 56 islands, the most important are Itaparica, Madre de Deus, Maré, Frades, Medo, Bom Jesus dos Passos.

Dendê Coast

The Dendê Coast, south of Salvador, is surrounded by verdant vegetation, clear waters, islands, bays, coral reefs and a very diversified fauna. It is connected to Salvador and the southern part of the state by ferryboats and the BA-001 highway, the second ecological highway along the Bahian coast, which connects the southern coastline and the extreme southern part of the state. It includes the municipalities of Valença, Cairu and the International attractions of Morro de São Paulo, Camamu, Taperoá, Igrapiúna, Ituberá and Maraú. The mouth of the Rio Una, in the form of a delta, contains 26 islands, the largest of which is Tinharé, where the Morro de São Paulo is located. At Boipeba and Cairú, which are part of the archipelago of Tinharé, the diversity of the ecosystems enables visitors to practice water sports, walk along the beach, follow trails in the rainforest and bathe on completely deserted beaches such as Garapuá.

Morro de São Paulo.

Cacao Coast

Along the southern coast of Bahia, the Cacao Coast preserves ecological sanctuaries with dozens of kilometers of beaches shaded by dense coconut groves, the Atlantic Forest, large areas of wetland vegetation and cacao plantations, the great allies in the struggle to defend the preservation of the Atlantic Forest. Walking along paths in the forest or along the beaches, horseback riding along the coast, boat trips up the vast number of rivers are some of the options that the region offers. Here one can find Environmental Protection Areas at Itacaré/Serra Grande and the Lagoa Encantada in Ilhéus, the Biological Reserve of Una and the Ecological Reserve of Prainha at Itacaré. From the Morro de Pernambuco to Canavieiras, there are 110 km (68 mi) of beaches, some of them highly popular, and other deserted, with clear water, reefs, inlets, coconut grove and an infinite number of estuaries of rivers which extend throughout the Cacao Coast. Highway BA-001 links the municipalities, nearly always bordering the coastline. The most important locations at Cacao Coast are: Itacaré, Ilhéus, and Olivença.

The Discovery Coast

The Discovery Coast preserves, virtually intact, the landscape seen by the Portuguese fleet described in the first pages of the history of Brazil. There are approximately 150 km (93 mi) of beaches, inlets, bays, cliffs, numerous rivers and streams surrounded by the verdant coconut groves, wetlands and the Atlantic Forest. Over land and sea the excursions are always associated with nature, and there are various types of water sports, walks, trips on horseback, surfing and deep sea diving. Recife de Fora, Coroa Alta and Trancoso for one day schooner excursions. BA-001 and two ferryboat systems over the Rio João de Tiba and Rio Buranhém connect the municipalities with the coast.

Church in Porto Seguro.

Trips from Barra do Cai, passing through the Parque Nacional do Monte Pascoal, Caraíva, Trancoso, Arraial d'Ajuda, the environmental protection areas of Santo Antônio and Coroa Vermelha, to the mouth of the Rio João de Tiba as far as the Rio Jequitinhonha are among the various ecological trips for visitors.

The Whale Coast

The Abrolhos archipelago in the extreme southern part of Bahia is a ecotourism attraction for diving and whale watching. Whales are frequent between July and November. This region contains one of the largest concentrations of fish, in terms of volume and variety, per square meter on the planet. There are 17 species of corals. The Whale Coast includes the municipalities of Alcobaça, Caravelas, Nova Viçosa and Mucuri and its main attraction is the Abrolhos Marine National Park.

The Diamantina Tableland Region

The geographical center of Bahia is the Diamantina Tableland region. In this mountainous region with a diversified topography, 90% of the[rivers of the Paraguaçu, Jacuípe and Rio das Contas basins have their source here. There are thousands of kilometers of clear waters that spring from these mountains and descend in cascades and waterfalls to plateaus and plains, forming beautiful natural pools. The vegetation mixes cactus species of the caatinga dry lands with rare examples of the mountain flora, especially bromeliads, orchids and "sempre vivas" (member of the strawflower family). On the area one can find the three highest mountains in the state: Pico do Barbado, 2080 m (6820 ft) high, Pico Itobira, 1970 m (6460 ft), and Pico das Almas, 1958 m (6424 ft).

Chapada Diamantina.

Another scenic attraction is the Cachoeira da Fumaça (Waterfall), that falls 420 m (1380 ft), the Gruta dos Brejões, the largest cavern opening of Bahia, and the amazing Poço Encantado, which fascinates visitors to the region. There are so many natural attractions that it is possible to choose between subterranean routes in caves, or trip to waterfalls, trek along old gold mining trails or follow the steps of the Prestes Column, rappel, climb mountains, or go horseback riding in the Vale do Capão or Vale do Paty, in the midst of esoteric and alternative communities. Many of the sites are protected by the National Park of Diamantina Tableland region and the Environmental Preservation Area Serra do Barbado and Marimbus, Iraquara. There are opportunities to take long bikes, or travel on horseback, mountain bike or off-road vehicles.

Tourism and recreation

Bahia is the most important tourist center in the Northeast and the 2nd in the country. The tourist product in Bahia, 50% of its global flow centered in Salvador, unites in a same space the characteristics of a natural landscape and a unique culture in the country, in which the typical culinary arts, the colonial architecture and popular feasts reveal a strong integration of elements of European and African origin in the formation and in the way of life of the people of Bahia. By its natural and historic-cultural attractions, Bahia presents an enormous potential for the development of the tourist activity. Owner of the biggest portion of seacoast of the country and of singular views in its interior, Bahia possesses specific cultural, folklore and religious characteristics, manifest in its extensive calendar of popular festivities, in its architectonic patrimony and in its typical food.

Beach in Itacaré.

Salvador, with its Historical Center registered by UNESCO as a World Heritage Site and with its coast clipped into many beaches and dozens of islands, has a varied receptive infrastructure, composed of 170 hostelry units (of which 20 are of international standard hotels) and 25 thousand[beds, further to restaurants, bars, nightclubs, shopping malls, theaters, crafts centers, Convention and Fairs Center, rental agencies, tourist agencies, and other equipment and services. In the last few years, the State Government promoted the total restoration of the Pelourinho, the biggest set of colonial style buildings in Latin America, today transformed into an important point for visitation by tourists, that will find there a synthesis of what best Bahia has to offer in specialized services, in regional and international cooking, in architecture of the 17th and 18th centuries and in music, with daily shows by the great artists of Bahia, famous in the country and abroad. The period of popular festivities in Bahia has its high point between December and March (summer months) and has in carnival its supreme point, with more than one million tourists in Salvador, Porto Seguro and other cities of the State's Tourist circuit.

Education

Educational institutions

- Universidade Federal da Bahia (UFBA) (Federal University of Bahia);
- Universidade Católica de Salvador [7] (UCSal) (Catholic University of Salvador);
- Centro Federal de Educação Tecnológica da Bahia [8] (Cefet-BA);
- Escola Baiana de Medicina e Saúde Pública [9] (EBMSP) (Bahiana School of Medicine and Public Health);
- Universidade Salvador [10] (Unifacs) (Salvador University);
- Universidade Federal do Recôncavo da Bahia [11] (UFRB) (Federal University of Recôncavo da Bahia);
- Universidade Estadual do Sudoeste da Bahia [12] (Uesb) (State University of Southwest of Bahia);
- Universidade Estadual de Santa Cruz [13] (UESC) (State University of Santa Cruz);
- Universidade do Estado da Bahia [14] (Uneb) (University of State of Bahia);
- Universidade Estadual de Feira de Santana [15] (UEFS) (State University of Feira de Santana);
- Fundação Universidade Federal do Vale do São Francisco [16] (UNIVASF) (Foundation Federal University of São Francisco Valley);
- Centro Universitário da Bahia [17] (FIB) (University Centre of Bahia);
- and many others.

Thales de Azevedo State High School.

Universidade Estadual de Feira de Santana.

Culture

As the chief locus of the early Brazilian slave trade, Bahia is considered to possess the greatest and most distinctive African imprint, in terms of culture and customs, in Brazil. These include the Yoruba-derived religious system of Candomblé, the martial art of capoeira, African-derived music such as samba (especially samba's Bahian precursor samba-de-roda), afoxé, and axé, and a cuisine with strong links to western Africa.

Capoeira in Salvador.

Bahia is the birthplace of many noted Brazilian artists, writers and musicians. Among the noted musical figures born in the state are Dorival Caymmi; João Gilberto; Gilberto Gil, the former (2003–2008) country's Minister of Culture; Caetano Veloso and his sister Maria Bethânia (Gil and Veloso being the founders of the Tropicália movement (a native adaptation of the hippie movement) of the late 1960s and early 1970s, which ultimate gained international recognition); Gal Costa; Luis Caldas; Sara Jane; Daniela Mercury; Ivete Sangalo; Carlinhos Brown and Margareth Menezes.

The city of Salvador is also home to famous groups known as "blocos-afros", including Olodum, Ara Ketu, É o Tchan, and Ilê Aiyê. Additionally, groups such as Chiclete com Banana also are based in Bahia. The first well-known rock'n roll singer in Brazil was also from Bahia. Born Raul Seixas, he was known as "Maluco Beleza" or "Peaceful Lunatic" (being "beleza (beauty)" in this manner means to be either "in peace" or "tranquil").

During the 19th century, one of Brazil's greatest poets, the Bahian abolitionist poet and playwright Castro Alves, a native of the *recôncavo* city of Cachoeira, penned his most famous poem, *Navio negreiro*, about slavery; the poem is considered a masterpiece of Brazilian Romanticism and a central anti-slavery text.

Nowadays, there are about 50 museums in Salvador alone, of which 25 are functioning normally.

Other notable Bahian writers include playwright and screenwriter Dias Gomes, Gregório de Matos, who wrote during the 17th century and was one of the first Brazilian writers, and Fr. Antonio Vieira, who during the colonial period was one of many authors who contributed to the expansion of the Portuguese language throughout the Brazilian territory.

The major Brazilian fiction writer of the 20th century, Jorge Amado, was born in the southeastern Bahian city of Itabuna, and resided for many years in Salvador. His major novels include *Gabriela, Cinnamon and Cloves*; *Dona Flor and Her Two Husbands*; and *Tieta, the Goat Girl*, all of which became internationally renowned films. More recent writers from Bahia include the fiction writers João Ubaldo Ribeiro and Jean Wyllys, winner of *Big Brother Brasil* 5 in 2005. In the visual and plastic arts, one of the best known Bahian figures was the multigenre artist and Argentinian native Hector Julio Páride Bernabó, also known as Carybé (1911–1997). Fine examples of his work are visible in the Afro-Brazilian Museum in Salvador.

Colonial Portuguese architecture in Pelourinho, Salvador.

Carnival

Preparing for Carnival in Salvador.

Like river rapids, from which no one wants to escape, the 'Trio-Elétricos' sweep up whoever is in Salvador during Carnival. The 'Trio-Elétricos', floats with amplifiers used as moving stages, pass through three official circuits. Behind them, more than 2 million merrymakers dance along 25 km (16 mi) of streets and avenues. Osmar's float goes from Campo Grande to Castro Alves square, in the town centre; Dodô's float, goes from Farol da Barra to Ondina, along the coast; and Batatinha's float goes across the Pelourinho. The first is the oldest circuit. It is also where the event's most traditional groups parade. In the Dodô circuit, where the more famous artists' box seats are located, the party becomes lively toward the end of the afternoon, and it continues like this until morning.

Infrastructure

International airport

Dep. Luís Eduardo Magalhães International Airport is located in an area of more than 6 million square meters (1500 acres) between sand dunes and native vegetation. The road route to the airport has already become one of the city's main scenic attractions. And lies 20 km (12 mi) north of Downtown Salvador. In 2007, the airport handled 5,920,573 passengers and 91,043 aircraft movements,[18] placing it 5th busiest airport in Brazil in terms of passengers. The airport's use has been growing at an average of 14% a year and now is responsible for more than 30% of passenger movement in Northeastern Brazil. Nearly 35 thousand people circulate daily through the passenger terminal. The airport generates more than 16 thousand direct and indirect jobs, to serve a daily average of over 10 thousand passengers, 250 takeoffs and landings of 100 domestic and 16 international flights.

Deputado Luís Eduardo Magalhães International Airport (SSA).

There are good cafes and fast food restaurants at the airport. A bar offers alcoholic or soft drinks. There are several shops in the terminal building selling a variety of items, including fashion clothing, jewellery, gift items and books and magazines. There is also a pharmacy in the terminal building. Buses between the city centre and the airport are fairly frequent. Take the Praça da Sé (Sé Square)/Aeroporto bus. It is much cheaper than going by taxi. Buses also go to Rodoviária (bus terminal), which is the city's main bus station and located 5 km (3.1 mi) from the city centre. The car park of the airport, is located near the terminal building and has parking spaces for 600 cars.

The International Airlines are: Lufthansa, TAP, United Airlines, American Airlines, Alitália, Air France, Air Europa, Ibéria, Aerolíneas Argentinas, LanChile. In addition to domestic and regional services, the airport has non-stop flights to Lisbon, Madrid, Frankfurt, Montevideo, London, Santiago, Buenos Aires, Asunción and Miami. Its IATA airport code is SSA and it is the sixth busiest airport in the country, the first in northeastern Brazil, behind Congonhas International, Guarulhos International, Juscelino Kubitschek International, Santos Dumont Regional and Galeão International.

Highways

BA- 001, BR-101, BR-116, BR-242, BR-251, BR-324, BR-342, BR-367, BR-407, BR-418, BR-420, BR-445, BR-498.

Bahia's government is also inaugurating a large portion of the BA 001 between Morro de São Paulo and Itacare. The constructions began in September 2006 and it's scheduled to finish mid-2009. That portion of the highway will allow travelers to save up to two hours on a trip from Salvador to Ilheus or Itacare. It was a controversial part of the constructions since a small portion of native rain forest had to be destroyed. However, the IBAMA (Brazilian Institute of Environment and Renewable Natural Resources) followed closely the development of the road and the harm to the forest was minimal. The new part of the BA 001 will benefit thousands of families that live near the highway will be benefited with transportation, schools and will exponentially enhance tourism in Itacare, Camamu and Ilheus.

Linha Verde Highway.

The plan is to ultimately connect Bahia's coast from north to south entirely through BA-001.

Port

With cargo volume that grows year after year following the same economic development rhythm implemented in the State, the Port of Salvador, located in the Bahia de Todos os Santos, holds status as the port with the highest movement of containers of the North/Northeast and the second-leading fruit exporter in Brazil. The port's facilities operate from 8am to noon and from 1h30am to 5h30pm.

The ability to handle high shipping volume has positioned the port of Salvador for new investments in technological modernization, and the port is noted for implementing a high level of operational flexibility and competitive rates. The goal of port officials is to offer the necessary infrastructure for the movement of goods, while simultaneously meeting the needs of international importers and exporters.

Investments

The State of Bahia has been assigning a significant part of its revenues to public investments. The investment programs of the state have been backed basically by its own resources and, in a complementary fashion, with resources originating from credit operations signed with international organizations (World Bank, IDB, KFW, OECF, etc.), and with national creditors (CEF, BNDES, etc.). There are governmental investments in progress in the fields of environmental and urban sanitation (Bahia Azul), popular housing (Viver Melhor), transportation (Corredores Rodoviários), tourism (Prodetur), urban development (Produr), and regional development (Sertão Forte).

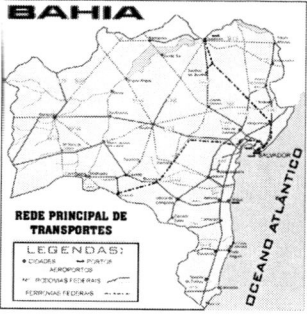

Transports in the state.

The airports of the State received special attention from the Government, with the development of a systematic program of reforms and improvements of the small airports of the interior, and, simultaneously, with the construction and/or improvements of the airports of the regions with some tourist appeal. Some distinction must be given in this work, for instance, to the construction of the airports of Piritiba and Mimoso do Oeste, in Barreiras region, both finished by now. To the landing runway and marshalling yard enlargements of the Porto Seguro Airport, enabling it to receive large aircraft like the 767-400 Boeing. To the construction (in progress) of two new airports in the interior: one in Valença, near Morro de São Paulo, and the other in Lençóis, in the Diamantina Tableland region; also to some repairs and improvements of the airports of Jequié, Irecê, Barreiras, Feira de Santana and Esplanada, among many others.

The Government policy for transportation, has emphasized the integration of different transportation systems aiming to facilitate the flow of production, to reduce costs and to increase the competitiveness of the Bahian economy. For this purpose, the Government has conceived and is already implementing the "Corredor Intermodal de Transporte" (an intermodal transportation system), situated in the São Francisco River, that combines in one system waterways, roads and a railway. The system connects all the sailable part of the river (1371 km (852 mi) within the State) to many roads and to one railroad, the "Centro Atlântica". This system conducts to the Salvador and Aratu ports all the economic production of the West and São Francisco regions, at a reduced cost.

State University of Bahia in Caetité.

Social areas have also been given priority by current and previous administrations. The construction of new teaching facilities, the set up of a training and career development center for teachers, as well as new hospitals and health centers, and the acquisition of equipment and the modernization of the civil and military polices are examples of this

Government's action. The significant increase in the amount of investments in the year 1997 is explained by the success of the state privatization program, confirming the purpose of the government in intensifying public development projects throughout the state. The State of Bahia has the best Human Development Index of Northeastern Brazil.

Sports

Football (*soccer* in the US) is the most popular sport. The two most popular football teams are Esporte Clube Bahia and Esporte Clube Ypiranga. In 2011, Bahia plays in the Brazilian Championship Serie A (first division/premier league), while Vitoria plays in the Brazilian Championship Serie B (second division). Bahia has won the two most important football national league: The Taça Brasil in 1959 and the Brazilian Championship Serie A (Campeonato Brasileiro) in 1988. Vitoria has never been a national champion but was runner up of the Brazilian Serie A in 1993.

In the sport of boxing, Bahian native Acelino "Popó" Freitas has been world champion (WBC) in the lightweight class. Other prominent fighters from this state are former heavyweight champion of both Pride Fighting Championship and Ultimate Fighting Championship Antônio Rodrigo Nogueira and his twin brother Antônio Rogério Nogueira.

Salvador is one of the host cities of the 2014 FIFA World Cup, for which Brazil is the host nation.

Further reading

- Anadelia A. Romo. *Brazil's Living Museum: Race, Reform, and Tradition in Bahia* (University of North Carolina Press; 2010) 221 pages; explores the shifting identity of the northeastern state of Bahia, which has a majority Afro-Brazilian population; covers the period from the abolition of slavery, in 1888, to the start of Brazil's military regime, in 1964.

References

[1] Censo 2010: população do Brasil é de 190.732.694 pessoas (http://www.ibge.gov.br/home/presidencia/noticias/noticia_visualiza. php?id_noticia=1766&id_pagina=1)
[2] http://www.bahia.ba.gov.br/
[3] In Brazilian Portuguese. In European Portuguese the pronunciation is [bɐˈi.ɐ]. The H is not pronounced, and the stress is on the *i*.
[4] PNAD.
[5] (in Portuguese) (PDF). Bahia, Brazil: IBGE. 2008. ISBN 85-240-3919-1. http://www.sidra.ibge.gov.br/bda/tabela/listabl.asp?z=pnad&o=3&i=P&c=262. Retrieved 2010-01-18.
[6] (in Portuguese) (PDF) *List of Brazilian states by GDP* (http://en.wikipedia.org/wiki/List_of_Brazilian_states_by_GDP_participation). Bahia, Brazil: IBGE. 2004. ISBN 85-240-3919-1. . Retrieved 2007-07-18.
[7] http://www.ucsal.br/
[8] http://www.cefetba.br/
[9] http://www.fundeci.com.br/
[10] http://www.unifacs.br/main/capa/default.aspx
[11] http://www.ufrb.edu.br/portal/
[12] http://www.uesb.br/
[13] http://www.uesc.br/
[14] http://www.uneb.br/
[15] http://www.uefs.br/portal
[16] http://www.univasf.edu.br/
[17] http://www.fib.br/
[18] Airport statistics for 2007 (Infraero) - Deputado Luís Eduardo Magalhães International Airport (http://www.infraero.gov.br/upload/arquivos/movi/mov.operac.1207.pdf)

External links

- (Portuguese) History of Bahia (http://www.visiteabahia.com.br/visite/historiadabahia/)
- (Portuguese) Geography of Bahia (http://www.bahiaemfoco.com/bahia/geografia.html)
- (Portuguese) Population of Bahia (http://www.ibge.gov.br/home/estatistica/populacao/censo2000/universo.php?tipo=31o/tabela13_1.shtm&paginaatual=1&uf=29&letra=A)

Alberto_Santos-Dumont

Alberto Santos-Dumont	

Born	July 20, 1873Palmira, Minas Gerais, Empire of Brazil
Died	July 23, 1932 (aged 59)Guarujá, São Paulo, Brazil
Occupation	Aviator, Inventor
Signature	

Alberto Santos-Dumont (Portuguese pronunciation: [ˈsẽtus duˈmõw̃]; July 20, 1873 – July 23, 1932), was a Brazilian early pioneer of aviation. The heir of a wealthy family of coffee producers, Santos Dumont dedicated himself to science studies in Paris, France, where he spent most of his adult life.

Santos-Dumont designed, built and flew one of the first practical dirigibles. In doing so he demonstrated that routine, controlled flight was possible. This "conquest of the air", in particular his winning the Deutsch de la Meurthe prize on October 19, 1901 on a flight that rounded the Eiffel Tower,[1] made him one of the most famous people in the world during the early 20th century.

In addition to his pioneering work in airships, Santos-Dumont made the first European public flight of an airplane on October 23, 1906. Designated *14-bis* or *Oiseau de proie* (French for "bird of prey"), the flying machine was the first fixed-wing aircraft witnessed by the European press and French aviation authorities to take off and successfully fly. Santos-Dumont is considered the "Father of Aviation" in Brazil, his native country.[2] His flight is the first to have been certified by the *Aéro Club de France* and the *Fédération Aéronautique Internationale (FAI)*.[3] [4]

Caricature of Santos-Dumont from Vanity Fair, 1899

Santos-Dumont occupied the 38th chair of the Brazilian Academy of Letters, from 1931 until his death in 1932.

Childhood

Santos-Dumont was born in Cabangu Farm, a farm in the Brazilian town of Palmira, today named Santos Dumont in the state of Minas Gerais, in the Southeast Brazil. He grew up as the sixth of eight children on a coffee plantation owned by his family in the state of São Paulo. His French-born father was an engineer, and made extensive use of the latest labor-saving inventions on his vast property. So successful were these innovations that Santos-Dumont's father gathered a large fortune and became known as the "Coffee King of Brazil."

He was fascinated by machinery, and while still a young child he learned to drive the steam tractors and locomotive used on his family's plantation. He was also a fan of Jules Verne and had read all his books before his tenth birthday. He wrote in his autobiography that the dream of flying came to him while contemplating the magnificent skies of Brazil in the long, sunny afternoons at the plantation.

According to the custom of wealthy families of the time, after receiving basic instruction at home with private instructors including his parents, young Alberto was sent out alone to larger cities to do his secondary studies. He studied for a while in "Colégio Culto à Ciência", in Campinas.

Move to France

In 1891, Alberto's father had an accident while inspecting some machinery. He fell from his horse and became a paraplegic. He decided to sell the plantation and move to Europe with his wife and younger children. At 17, Santos-Dumont left the prestigious Escola de Minas in Ouro Preto, Minas Gerais, for Paris. Shortly after he arrived, he bought an automobile. Later, he pursued studies in physics, chemistry, mechanics, and electricity with the help of a private tutor.

Balloons and dirigibles

Santos-Dumont #6 rounding the Eiffel Tower in the process of winning the Deutsch Prize. Photo courtesy of the Smithsonian Institution (SI Neg. No. 85-3941)

Santos-Dumont described himself as the first "sportsman of the air." He started flying by hiring an experienced balloon pilot and took his first balloon rides as a passenger. He quickly moved on to piloting balloons himself, and shortly thereafter to designing his own balloons. In 1898, Santos-Dumont flew his first balloon design, the *Brésil*.

After numerous balloon flights, he turned to the design of steerable balloons, known as *dirigibles*, that could be propelled through the air rather than drifting along with the wind. Between 1898 and 1905, he built and flew 11 dirigibles. With air traffic control restrictions still decades in the future, he would float along Paris boulevards at rooftop level in one of his airships, commonly landing in front of a fashionable outdoor cafe for lunch. On one occasion he even flew an airship early one morning to his own apartment at No. 9, Rue Washington, just off Avenue des Champs-Élysées, not far from the Arc de Triomphe.

To win the Deutsch de la Meurthe prize Santos-Dumont decided to build a bigger craft, the dirigible Number 5. On August 8, 1901 during one of his attempts, his dirigible lost hydrogen gas. It started to descend and was unable to clear the roof of the Trocadero Hotel. A loud explosion was then heard. Santos-Dumont survived the explosion and was left hanging in a basket from the side of the hotel. With the help of the crowd he climbed to the roof without injury.

The zenith of his lighter-than-air career came when he won the *Deutsch de la Meurthe* prize. The challenge called for a flight from the Parc Saint Cloud to the Eiffel Tower and back in less than thirty minutes. The winner of the prize needed to maintain an average ground speed of at least 22 km/h (14 mph) to cover the round trip distance of 11 km (6.8 mi) in the allotted time.

On October 19, 1901, after several attempts, Santos-Dumont succeeded in using his dirigible *Number 6*. Immediately after the flight, a controversy broke out around a last minute rule change regarding the precise timing of the flight. There was much public outcry and comment in the press. Finally, after several days of vacillating by the committee of officials, Santos-Dumont was awarded the prize as well as the prize money of 125,000 francs. In a charitable gesture, he donated 75,000 francs of the prize money to the poor of Paris. The balance was given to his workmen as a bonus. An additional matching 125,000 francs was voted to him along with a gold medal by the government of his native Brazil.

Aida D'Acosta Breckinridge piloted Santos-Dumont's airship in 1903.

Santos-Dumont's aviation feats made him a celebrity in Europe and throughout the world. He won several more prizes and became a friend to millionaires, aviation pioneers, and royalty. In 1903 Aida D'Acosta Breckinridge piloted Santos-Dumont's airship. In 1904, he went to the United States and was invited to the White House to meet U.S. President Theodore Roosevelt.

In 1904, Santos-Dumont shipped his new airship No. 7 (also called Racer), to St. Louis from Paris in several crates to fly at the Louisiana Purchase Exposition. It was a new airship, built to compete for the Grand Prize of $100,000, which was to be given to a flying machine (of any sort) that could make three round-trip flights over a 15-mile "L"-shaped course at an overall average speed of 20 miles/hour (later reduced to 15 miles/hour). It was also necessary for the machine to land without damage (to craft or crew) not more than fifty yards from the starting point. Because he was probably the best-known aviator at the time, the Fair committee went to great lengths to ensure his participation, including modifying the rules. However, upon arrival in St. Louis, Santos-Dumont found his airship's gas bag to be irreparably damaged; sabotage, although suspected, was never proven, and Santos-Dumont did not participate in the contest. In fact, suspicion of the deed, a repeat of a similar incident in Boston, began to focus somewhat absurdly on Santos-Dumont himself, and he indignantly left the Fair and returned immediately to France.

The public eagerly followed his daring exploits. Parisians affectionately dubbed him *le petit Santos*. The fashionable folk of the day mimicked various aspects of his style of dress from his high collared shirts to his signature Panama hat. He was, and remains to this day, a prominent folk hero in his native Brazil.

Heavier than air aircraft

Although Santos-Dumont continued to work on dirigibles, his primary interest soon turned to heavier-than-air aircraft. By 1905 he had finished his first airplane design, and also a helicopter. He finally achieved his dream of flying an aircraft on October 23, 1906 by piloting the 14-bis before a large crowd of witnesses for a distance of 60 metres (197 ft) at a height of two to three metres (10 ft). This well-documented event was the first flight verified by the Aéro-Club de France of a powered heavier-than-air machine in Europe and won the Deutsch-Archdeacon Price for the first officially observed flight

The November 12 flight.

further than 25 meters. On November 12, 1906, Santos-Dumont set the first world record recognized by the Federation Aeronautique Internationale by flying 220 metres in 21.5 seconds.[5][6]

Santos-Dumont made other contributions to the field of aircraft design. He added movable surfaces, the precursor to ailerons, between the wings in an effort to gain more lateral stability than was offered by the *14-bis* wing dihedral. He also pushed for and exploited substantial improvements in engine power-to-weight ratio, and other refinements in aircraft construction techniques.

Alberto Santos-Dumont flying the Demoiselle over Paris

Santos-Dumont's final design were the Demoiselle monoplanes (Nos. 19 to 22). This aircraft was employed as Dumont's personal transportation and he willingly let others make use of his design. The fuselage consisted of three specially reinforced bamboo booms, and the pilot sat a seat between the main wheels of a tricycle landing gear. The Demoiselle was controlled in flight by a tail unit that functioned both as elevator and rudder, and by wing warping (No. 20).

In 1908 Santos-Dumont started working with Adolphe Clément's Clement-Bayard company to build the *Demoiselle No 19*. They planned a production run of 100 units, built 50 and sold only 15 for 7,500 francs for each airframe. It was the world's first series production aircraft. By 1909 it was offered with a choice of 3 engines, Clement 20 hp; Wright 4-cyl 30 hp (Clement-Bayard had the license to manufacture Wright engines); and Clement-Bayard 40 hp designed by Pierre Clerget. The Demoiselle achieved 120 km/h.[7]

The Demoiselle airplane could be constructed in only 15 days. Possessing outstanding performance, easily covering 200 m of ground during the initial flights and flying at speeds of more than 100 km/h, the Demoiselle was the last aircraft built by Santos-Dumont. The June 1910 edition of the Popular Mechanics magazine published drawings of the Demoiselle and affirmed that "This machine is better than any other which has ever been built, for those who wish to reach results with the least possible expense and with a minimum of experimenting." American companies sold drawings and parts for Demoiselles for several years afterwards. Santos-Dumont was so enthusiastic about aviation that he released the drawings of Demoiselle for free, thinking that aviation would be the mainstream of a new prosperous era for mankind.

The first fixed-wing aircraft: The *14-bis* versus the *Wright Flyers*

There is still controversy over whether the Wright 1903 Flyer I, or the 14-Bis was the first true airplane.

The Wrights used a launch catapult for their 1904 and 1905 machines, but the aircraft of Santos-Dumont and other Europeans had wheeled undercarriages. The Wright Brothers continued to use skids, which necessitated the use of a a dolly running on a track and the use of catapult in the absence of a headwind.

The Fédération Aéronautique Internationale, founded in France at the beginning of the century to verify aviation records, stated among its rules that an aircraft should be able to take off under its own power in order to qualify for a record. Supporters of Santos-Dumont's claim believe that this means the 14-bis was, technically, the first successful fixed-wing aircraft.

Flight of Santos Dumont, Le Petit Journal, 25 November 1906

Opinions vary on whether the Wright Flyer or the 14-bis was the more practical (and thus the "first") heavier-than-air flying machine. Both designs produced aircraft that made free, manned, powered flights. Which one was "first" or "more practical" is a matter of how those words are defined. No one could contest that the Wrights flew first or that Santos-Dumont took off on wheels before the Wrights and earned a variety of prizes and official records in France. Patriotic pride heavily influences opinions of the relative importance and practicality of each aircraft, thus causing debate. Americans prefer definitions that make the Wrights the

14-bis on an old postcard

"first" to fly, while Brazilians believe that Santos-Dumont had the first "real", practical aircraft, and that his nationality may have caused his accomplishments to not receive worldwide recognition.

Many other inventors could also claim to have produced the first flying machine. A long series of "flying machines" achieved some of the criteria that are required of an "aircraft." These achievements, most of them first accomplished in the 1800s, include being able to sustain flight using lighter-than-air craft, powered machines which could generate enough lift to rise off the ground, but which were not controllable, and unpowered winged vehicles that flew briefly and that could be controlled. For example, Frederick Marriott's Avitor was a slightly-heavier-than-air dirigible that was fully controllable. It relied primarily on a large hydrogen gas bag for flight, but it had wings and could only get off the ground by moving forward so that the wings generated the additional lift needed to overcome its weight. Could such a hybrid be "the first heavier-than-air flying machine"? It is only one of many examples of a long history of flying contraptions, so this debate could easily be extended well beyond being about simply the 14-Bis versus the Wright Flyer.[8]

Wristwatch

The wristwatch had already been invented by Patek Philippe, decades earlier, but Santos-Dumont played an important role in popularizing its use by men in the early 20th century. Before him they were generally worn only by women (as jewels), as men favoured pocket watches.

In 1904, while celebrating his winning of the Deutsch Prize at Maxim's Restaurant in Paris, Santos-Dumont complained to his friend Louis Cartier about the difficulty of checking his pocket watch to time his performance during flight. Santos-Dumont then asked Cartier to come up with an alternative that would allow him to keep both hands on the controls. Cartier went to work on the problem and the result was a watch with a leather band and a small buckle, to be worn on the wrist.[9]

Santos-Dumont never took off again without his personal Cartier wristwatch, and he used it to check his personal record for a 220 m (730 ft) flight, achieved in 21 seconds, on November 12, 1906. The Santos-Dumont watch was officially displayed on October 20, 1979 at the Paris Air Museum next to the 1908 *Demoiselle*, the last aircraft that he built.

Later years

Santos-Dumont bought one of the very early Le Zèbre cars, now on display at the São Paulo car museum.

Santos-Dumont continued to build and fly airplanes. His final flight as a pilot was made in Demoiselle on January 4, 1910. The flight ended in an accident, but the cause was never completely clear. There were few observers and no reporters on the scene. However, in a PBS documentary about Santos-Dumont it is alleged that the crash was due to a snapped wire.[10]

Santos-Dumont fell seriously ill a few months later. He experienced double vision and vertigo that made it impossible for him to drive, much less fly. He was diagnosed with multiple sclerosis. He abruptly dismissed his staff and closed his workshop. His illness soon led to a deepening depression.

In 1911, Santos-Dumont moved from Paris to the French seaside village of Bénerville (now Benerville-sur-Mer) where he took up astronomy as a hobby. Some of the local folk, who knew little of his great fame and exploits in Paris just a few years earlier, mistook his German-made telescope and unusual accent as signs that he was a German spy who was tracking French naval activity. These suspicions eventually led to Santos-Dumont having his rooms searched by the French military police. Upset by the charge, as well as depressed from his illness, he burned all of his papers, plans, and notes. Thus, there is little direct information available about his designs today.

In 1918 (some sources report 1916), he left France to go back to his country of birth, never to return to Europe. His return to Brazil was marred by tragedy. A dozen members of the Brazilian scientific community boarded a seaplane with the intention of paying a flying welcome to the returning aviator on the luxury liner *Cap Arcona*. Instead, the seaplane crashed with the loss of all on board. The loss deepened Santos-Dumont's growing despondency.

In Brazil, Santos-Dumont bought a small lot on the side of a hill in the city of Petrópolis, in the mountains near Rio de Janeiro, and in 1918 built a small house there filled with imaginative mechanical gadgetry including an alcohol-fueled heated shower of his own design. The hill was purposefully chosen because of its great steepness as a proof that ingenuity could make it possible to build a comfortable house in that unlikely site. After building it, he used to spend his summers there to escape the heat in Rio, and affectionately called it *A Encantada* (*The Enchanted*), after its street, *Rua do Encanto* (*Enchantment Street*). The house has its stairs designed in a curious way, each tread alternately hollowed in the right and left, like an alternating tread stair: it allows that the stairs be steep enough to fit the little room available in the house, but still enable people to climb it comfortably. As the first hollow was in the left side of the stairs, people must step first with their right foot to climb it.

"A Encantada", the house of Santos-Dumont in Petrópolis

Private life

Santos-Dumont, a lifelong bachelor, did seem to have a particular affection for a married Cuban-American woman named Aída de Acosta. She is the only person, other than himself, that he ever permitted to fly one of his airships. By allowing her to fly his No. 9 airship she most likely became the first woman to pilot a powered aircraft. Until the end of his life he kept a picture of her on his desk alongside a vase of fresh flowers. Nonetheless, there is no indication that Santos-Dumont and Acosta stayed in touch after her flight. Upon Santos-Dumont's death Acosta was reported as saying that she hardly knew the man.

He is also known to not only have often used an equal sign (=) between his two surnames in place of a hyphen, but also seems to have preferred that practice, to display equal respect for his father's French ethnicity and the Brazilian ethnicity of his mother.[11]

Death

Alberto Santos-Dumont – seriously ill, and said to be depressed over his multiple sclerosis(not confirmed) and the use of aircraft in warfare – is believed to have committed suicide by hanging himself in the city of Guarujá in São Paulo, on July 23, 1932. He was buried in the Cemitério São João Batista in Rio de Janeiro. There are many monuments commemorating him in the country of his birth and elsewhere. His house in Petrópolis, Brazil is now a museum.[12]

Legacy

- Santos Dumont is a small lunar impact crater that lies in the northern end of the Montes Apenninus range at the eastern edge of the Mare Imbrium
- The aviator gives his name to the city of Santos Dumont, in the state of Minas Gerais, Brazil. In this municipality is located the Cabangu farm, where he was born. The Faculdades Santos Dumont is a group of private higher learning colleges in the city.[13]
- The city of Dumont, in the state of São Paulo, near Ribeirão Preto is so named because it is located where it used to be one the largest coffee farms in the world, between 1870 and 1890. The farm was owned by Alberto Santos-Dumont's father. It was sold in 1896 to a British company, the *Dumont Coffee Company*.
- The airport for domestic flights of Rio de Janeiro is also named after him (see Santos Dumont Regional Airport)
- The Rodovia Santos Dumont is a highway in the state of São Paulo.
- The Brazilian Air Force (Command of Aeronautics) awards the Santos Dumont Medal of Merit to important personalities in the world of aviation. The state government of Minas Gerais has a similar medal.
- The *Réseau Santos Dumont* is a cooperative university network between France and Brazil, instituted by the French and Brazilian Ministries of Education in 1994, with 26 universities in each country.
- The American Office of Naval Research of San Diego, California named one of its research airships as the *600B Santos Dumont*.[14]
- The Historic and Cultural Institute of Aeronautics of Brazil has instituted the Santos Dumont Annual Prize of Journalism to the best reports in the media about aeronautics.
- The Lycée Polyvalent Santos Dumont is a lyceum in Saint-Cloud, France[15]
- Tens of thousands of streets, avenues, plazas, schools, monuments, etc., are dedicated to the national hero in Brazil.
- He is mentioned as a pioneer of aviation, specifically in the area of dirigibles, in the 1984 novel by Robert A. Heinlein entitled Job: A Comedy of Justice.
- The official Brazilian Presidential Aircraft, an Airbus Corporate Jet tail number FAB2101, was named Alberto Santos Dumont.
- A popular Chilean rock band of the 1990s adopted the name Santos Dumont.[16]

Bust near the Brazilian Embassy, Washington, D.C., USA

Ice cream made by the Santos Dumont Coffee Company.

- A short story by H.G. Wells, "The Truth About Pyecraft", includes a reference to Santos Dumont and his skill as an aviator.
- The aviator gives his name to a boutique Aircraft Management and Consultancy Company, Santos Dumont, founded in May 2004.

See also

- First flying machine
- Airship
- Aviation history
- List of early flying machines
- List of firsts in aviation
- List of Santos-Dumont aircraft
- List of years in aviation
- History of watches
- History of timekeeping devices

References

Notes

[1] "M. Santos Dumont Rounds Eiffel Tower." (http://query.nytimes.com/mem/archive-free/pdf?_r=1& res=9B00E3DF1430E033A25753C2A9669D946097D6CF) *The New York Times*, October 20, 1901. Retrieved: January 12, 2009.
[2] Hansen 2005, p. 299.
[3] Les vols du 14bis relatés au fil des éditions du journal l'illustration de 1906. (http://www.aeroclub.com/santos_dumont_14bis_14bis.htm) The wording is: "cette prouesse est le premier vol au monde **homologué** par l'Aéro-Club de France et la toute jeune Fédération Aéronautique Internationale (FAI)."
[4] Santos-Dumont: Pionnier de l'aviation, dandy de la Belle Epoque. (http://www.aeroclub.com/santos_dumont_14bis_index.htm)
[5] Jines. Ernest. "Santos Dumont in France 1906-1916: The Very Earliest Early Birds." (http://earlyaviators.com/edumonb.htm) *earlyaviators.com*, December 25, 2006. Retrieved: August 17, 2009.
[6] "Cronologia de Santos Dumont" (in Portugese). (http://santos-dumont.net/indexcronologia.html) *santos-dumont.net*. Retrieved: October 12, 2010.
[7] Hartmann, Gérard. "Clément-Bayard, sans peur et sans reproche" (French). (http://www.hydroretro.net/etudegh/clement-bayard.pdf) *hydroretro.net*. Retrieved: November 14, 2010.
[8] "Avitor." (http://www.webcitation.org/5uEak0k0a) *Hiller Aviation Museum*, 2007. Retrieved: November 14, 2010.
[9] "Aviation Pioneer Scored A First in Watch-Wearing." *The New York Times*, October 25, 1975. Retrieved: July 21, 2009.
[10] "NOVA 124: Wings of Madness." (http://www.pbs.org/wgbh/nova/santos/) *PBS*. Retrieved: November 14, 2010.
[11] Gray, Carroll F. (November 2006). "The 1906 Santos=Dumont No. 14bis". *World War I Aeroplanes* **No. 194**: 4.
[12] "Alberto Santos Dumont Lies In State in Brazil's Capital." *The New York Times*, December 19, 1932.
[13] "FESJ - Fundação Educacional São José." (http://www.fsd.edu.br) *www.fsd.edu.br*. Retrieved: August 9, 2010.
[14] "Airship Santos Dumont to Conduct Test Phase." (http://www.news.navy.mil/search/display.asp?story_id=9377) *www.news.navy.mil*. Retrieved: August 9, 2010.
[15] "Saint-Cloud." (http://www.ac-versailles.fr/etabliss/santos_stcloud/default1.htm) *ac-versailles.fr*.
[16] "Santos Dumont." (http://www.musicapopular.cl/2.0/index2.php?op=Artista&id=351) *musicapopular.cl*. Retrieved: August 9, 2010.

Bibliography

- de Barros, Henrique Lins. *Santos Dumont and the Invention of the Airplane* (PDF). (http://www.cbpf.br/ Publicacoes/SantosDumontINGLES.pdf) Rio de Janeiro: Brazilian Ministry of Science & Technology and the Brazilian Centre for Research in Physics, 2006. ISBN 978-85-85752-17-0.
- de Mattos, Bento S. "Santos Dumont and the Dawn of Aviation." *AIAA paper # 2004-106*, 42nd AIAA Aerospace Sciences Meeting and Exhibit, Reno, Nevada, January 2004.
- de Mattos, Bento S. "Short History of Brazilian Aeronautics." *AIAA paper # 2006-328*, 44th AIAA Aerospace Sciences Meeting and Exhibit, Reno, Nevada, January 2006.

- Garrett, Charles Hall. "A Builder of Successful Air-Ships". *The World's Work: A History of Our Time*, VIII, May 1904: pp. 4737–4739.
- Gray, Carroll F. "The 1906 Santos=Dumont No. 14bis". *World War I Aeroplanes*, Issue #194, November 2006, pgs. 4-21.
- Hansen, James R. *First Man: The Life of Neil Armstrong*. New York: Simon & Schuster, 2005. ISBN 978-0-7432-5631-5.
- Hoffman, Paul. *Wings of Madness: Alberto Santos Dumont and the Invention of Flight*. New York: Hyperion Press, 2003. ISBN 978-0-7868-6659-5.
- Santos Dumont, Alberto. *My Airships* (http://www.archive.org/details/myairships00santrich). London, G. Richards, 1904 hos / Follow Your Dreams: The Story of Alberto Santos Dumont), *(bilingual, Portuguese/English)*. Rio de Janeiro: Prometheus Press, 2005. *ISBN 978-85-99240-02-1*.
- Winters, Nancy. *Man Flies: The Story of Alberto Santos-Dumont, Master of the Balloon*. New York: Ecco Press, 1997. ISBN 978-0-88001-636-0.
- Wykeham, Peter. *Santos Dumont: A Study in Obsession*. New York: Harcourt, Brace & World, 1962. ISBN 978-0-405-12210-1.

External links

- U. S. Centennial of Flight Commission Dumont (http://www.centennialofflight.gov/essay/Dictionary/Santos-Dumont/DI41.htm)
- Alberto Santos Dumont (http://www.outsports.com/history/santosdumont.htm) Article by writer Patricia Nell Warren.
- History of Aviation: Brazil, American Institute of Aeronautics and Astronautics. (http://www.aiaa.org/content.cfm?pageid=432)
- Alberto Santos-Dumont (http://www.findagrave.com/cgi-bin/fg.cgi?page=gr&GRid=5381) at Find a Grave

Brazil

Federative Republic of Brazil República Federativa do Brasil (Portuguese)	

Motto: *"Ordem e Progresso"* (Portuguese) (English: "Order and Progress")	
Anthem: Hino Nacional Brasileiro (Portuguese) (English: Brazilian National Anthem)	
National seal Selo Nacional do Brasil (Portuguese) (English: "National Seal of Brazil")	

Capital	Brasília 15°45′S 47°57′W
Largest city	São Paulo
Official language(s)	Portuguese[1]
Ethnic groups (2010[2])	47.73% White 43.13% Brown (Multiracial) 7.61% Black 1.09% Asian 0.43% Amerindian
Demonym	Brazilian
Government	Federal presidential constitutional republic

-	President	Dilma Rousseff (PT)
-	Vice President	Michel Temer (PMDB)
-	President of the Chamber of Deputies	Marco Maia (PT)
-	President of the Senate	José Sarney (PMDB)
-	Chief Justice	Cezar Peluso
	Legislature	National Congress
-	Upper House	Federal Senate
-	Lower House	Chamber of Deputies
	Independence	from United Kingdom of Portugal, Brazil and the Algarves
-	Declared	7 September 1822
-	Recognized	29 August 1825
-	Republic	15 November 1889
-	Current constitution	5 October 1988
	Area	
-	Total	8514877 km^2 (5th) 3287597 sq mi
-	Water (%)	0.65
	Population	
-	2011[3] estimate	192,376,496
-	2010 census	190,732,694[4] (5th)
-	Density	22/km^2 (182nd) 57/sq mi
GDP (PPP)		2011 estimate
-	Total	$2.309 trillion[5] (8th)
-	Per capita	$11,845[5] (75th)
GDP (nominal)		2011 estimate
-	Total	$2.518 trillion[6] (7th)
-	Per capita	$12,917[5] (53rd)
Gini (2010)		▽53.6[7]
HDI (2011)		0.718[8] (high) (84th)
	Currency	Real (R$) (BRL)
	Time zone	BRT[9] (UTC-2 to -4[9])
-	Summer (DST)	BRST (UTC-2 to -4)
	Date formats	dd/mm/yyyy (CE)
	Drives on the	right
	ISO 3166 code	BR
	Internet TLD	.br
	Calling code	+55

Brazil 🔊 /brəˈzɪl/ (Portuguese: *Brasil*, IPA: [bɾaˈziw]), officially the **Federative Republic of Brazil**[10] [11] (Portuguese: *República Federativa do Brasil*, listen), is the largest country in South America. It is the world's fifth largest country, both by geographical area and by population with over 192 million people.[12] [13] It is the only Portuguese-speaking country in the Americas and the largest lusophone country in the world.[12]

Bounded by the Atlantic Ocean on the east, Brazil has a coastline of 7491 km (4655 mi).[12] It is bordered on the north by Venezuela, Guyana, Suriname and the French overseas region of French Guiana; on the northwest by Colombia; on the west by Bolivia and Peru; on the southwest by Argentina and Paraguay and on the south by Uruguay. Numerous archipelagos form part of Brazilian territory, such as Fernando de Noronha, Rocas Atoll, Saint Peter and Paul Rocks, and Trindade and Martim Vaz.[12] It borders all other South American countries except Ecuador and Chile.

Brazil was a colony of Portugal from the landing of Pedro Álvares Cabral in 1500 until 1815, when it was elevated to the rank of kingdom and the United Kingdom of Portugal, Brazil and the Algarves was formed. The colonial bond was in fact broken in 1808, when the capital of the Portuguese colonial empire was transferred from Lisbon to Rio de Janeiro, after Napoleon invaded Portugal.[14] Independence was achieved in 1822 with the formation of the Empire of Brazil, a unitary state governed under a constitutional monarchy and a parliamentary system. The country became a presidential republic in 1889, when a military coup d'état proclaimed the Republic, although the bicameral legislature, now called Congress, dates back to the ratification of the first constitution in 1824.[14] Its current Constitution, formulated in 1988, defines Brazil as a Federal Republic.[15] The Federation is formed by the union of the Federal District, the 26 States, and the 5,564 Municipalities.[15] [16]

The Brazilian economy is the world's seventh largest by nominal GDP[6] and the eighth largest by purchasing power parity.[17] [18] Brazil is one of the world's fastest growing major economies. Economic reforms have given the country new international recognition.[19] Brazil is a founding member of the United Nations, the G20, CPLP, Latin Union, the Organization of Ibero-American States, the Organization of American States, Mercosul and the Union of South American Nations, and is one of the BRIC countries. Brazil is also home to diverse wildlife, natural environments, and extensive natural resources in a variety of protected habitats.[12]

Etymology

The word "Brazil" comes from brazilwood, a tree that once grew plentifully along the Brazilian coast. In Portuguese, brazilwood is called *pau-brasil*, with the word *brasil* commonly given the etymology "red like an ember", formed from Latin *brasa* ("ember") and the suffix *-il* (from *-iculum* or *-ilium*).[20] [21] [22] As brazilwood produces a deep red dye, it was highly valued by the European cloth industry and was the earliest commercially-exploited product from Brazil. Through the 16th century, massive amounts of brazilwood were harvested by indigenous peoples (mostly Tupi) along the Brazilian coast, who sold the timber to European traders (mostly Portuguese, but also French) in return for assorted European consumer goods. [23]

The official name of the land, in original Portuguese records, was the "Land of the Holy Cross (*Terra da Santa Cruz*), but European sailors and merchants commonly called it simply the "Land of Brazil" (*Terra do Brasil*) on account of the brazilwood trade. The popular appellation eclipsed and eventually supplanted the official name. Early sailors sometimes also called it the "Land of Parrots" (*Terra di Papaga*).

In the Guarani language, an official language of Paraguay, Brazil is called "Pindorama". This was the name the natives gave to the region, meaning "land of the palm trees".

History

Portuguese colonization

The land now called Brazil was claimed by Portugal in April 1500, on the arrival of the Portuguese fleet commanded by Pedro Álvares Cabral.[24] The Portuguese encountered stone age natives divided into several tribes, most of whom spoke languages of the Tupi–Guarani family, and fought among themselves.[25]

Though the first settlement was founded in 1532, colonization was effectively begun in 1534, when Dom João III divided the territory into twelve hereditary captaincies,[26] [27] but this arrangement proved problematic and in 1549 the king assigned a Governor-General to administer the entire colony.[27] [28] The Portuguese assimilated some of the native tribes[29] while others were enslaved or exterminated in long wars or by European diseases to which they had no immunity.[30] [31] By the mid-16th century, sugar had become Brazil's most important export[25] [32] and the Portuguese imported African slaves[33] [34] to cope with the increasing international demand.[30] [35]

The first Christian mass in Brazil, 1500.

Through wars against the French, the Portuguese slowly expanded their territory to the southeast, taking Rio de Janeiro in 1567, and to the northwest, taking São Luís in 1615.[36] They sent military expeditions to the Amazon rainforest and conquered British and Dutch strongholds,[37] founding villages and forts from 1669.[38] In 1680 they reached the far south and founded Sacramento on the bank of the Rio de la Plata, in the Eastern Strip region (present-day Uruguay).[39]

At the end of the 17th century, sugar exports started to decline[40] but beginning in the 1690s, the discovery of gold by explorers in the region that would later be called Minas Gerais (General Mines) in current Mato Grosso and Goiás, saved the colony from imminent collapse.[41] From all over Brazil, as well as from Portugal, thousands of immigrants came to the mines.[42]

The Spanish tried to prevent Portuguese expansion into the territory that belonged to them according to the 1494 Treaty of Tordesillas, and succeeded in conquering the Eastern Strip in 1777. However, this was in vain as the Treaty of San Ildefonso, signed in the same year, confirmed Portuguese sovereignty over all lands proceeding from its territorial expansion, thus creating most of the current Brazilian borders.[43]

In 1808, the Portuguese royal family and the majority of the Portuguese nobility, fleeing the troops of the French Emperor Napoleon I that were invading Portugal and most of Central Europe, established themselves in the city of Rio de Janeiro, which thus became the seat of the entire Portuguese Empire.[44] In 1815 Dom João VI, then regent on behalf of his incapacitated mother, elevated Brazil from colony to sovereign Kingdom united with Portugal.[44] In 1809 the Portuguese invaded French Guiana (which was returned to France in 1817)[45] and in 1816 the Eastern Strip, subsequently renamed Cisplatina.[46]

Independence and empire

After the Portuguese military had successfully repelled Napoleon's invasion, the King João VI returned to Europe on 26 April 1821, leaving his elder son Prince Pedro de Alcântara as regent to rule Brazil.[47] The Portuguese government, guided by the new political regime imposed by the Liberal Revolution of 1820, attempted to turn Brazil into a colony once again, thus depriving it of its achievements since 1808.[48] The Brazilians refused to yield and Prince Pedro stood

Declaration of the Brazilian independence by Emperor Pedro I on 7 September 1822.

by them declaring the country's independence from Portugal on 7 September 1822.[49] On 12 October 1822, Pedro was declared the first Emperor of Brazil and crowned Dom Pedro I on 1 December 1822.[50]

The public flogging of a slave in Rio de Janeiro. From Jean-Baptiste Debret, *Voyage Pittoresque et Historique au Bresil* (1834–1839).

At that time most Brazilians were in favour of a monarchy and republicanism had little support.[51] [52] The subsequent Brazilian War of Independence spread through almost the entire territory, with battles in the northern, northeastern, and southern regions.[53] The last Portuguese soldiers surrendered on 8 March 1824[54] and independence was recognized by Portugal on 29 August 1825.[55]

The first Brazilian constitution was promulgated on 25 March 1824, after its acceptance by the municipal councils across the country.[56] [57] [58] [59] Pedro I abdicated on 7 April 1831 and went to Europe to reclaim his daughter's crown, leaving behind his five year old son and heir, who was to become Dom Pedro II.[60] As the new emperor could not exert his constitutional prerogatives until he reached maturity, a regency was created.[61]

Disputes between political factions led to rebellions and an unstable, almost anarchical, regency.[62] It is estimated that from 30 to 40% of the population of the Province of Grão-Pará died during the Cabanagem revolt.[63] The rebellious factions, however, were not in revolt against the monarchy,[64] [65] even though some declared the secession of the provinces as independent republics, but only so long as Pedro II was a minor.[66] Because of this, Pedro II was prematurely declared of age and "Brazil was to enjoy nearly half a century of internal peace and rapid material progress."[67]

Despite the loss of Cisplatina in 1828 when it became an independent nation known as Uruguay,[68] Brazil won three international wars during the 58-year reign of Pedro II (the Platine War, the Uruguayan War and the War of the Triple Alliance, which left over 50,000 dead)[69] and witnessed the consolidation of representative democracy, mainly due to successive elections and unrestricted freedom of the press.[70] Most importantly, slavery was extinguished after a slow but steady process that began with the end of the international traffic in slaves in 1850[71] and ended with the complete abolition of slavery in 1888.[72] The slave population had been in decline since Brazil's independence: in 1823, 29% of the Brazilian population were slaves but by 1887 this had fallen to 5%.[73]

Brazilian forces (in blue uniform) engage the Paraguayan army (some in red uniform and other shirtless) during the War of the Triple Alliance.

When the monarchy was overthrown on 15 November 1889[74] there was little desire in Brazil to change the form of government[75] and Pedro II was at the height of his popularity among his subjects.[76] [77] However, he "bore prime, perhaps sole, responsibility for his own overthrow."[78] After the death of his two sons, Pedro believed that "the imperial regime was destined to end with him."[79] He cared little for the regime's fate[80] [81] and so neither did anything, nor allowed anyone else to do anything, to prevent the military coup, backed by former slave owners who resented the abolition of slavery.[82] [83] [84]

Early republic

At the beginning of the republican government it was little more than a military dictatorship,[74] and the new constitution restricted political rights, such as the right to vote,[85] [86] yet provided for direct elections to be held in 1894.[87] However, already in 1891, from the unfoldings of the encilhamento bubble[88] [89] and of the 1st naval revolt, the country entered in a prolonged cycle of financial, social and political instability, that would extend until the 1920s keeping the country plagued by several rebellions, both civilian[90] [91] [92] as military,[93] [94] [95] which little by little undermined the regime in a such extent, that by 1930 it was possible to the defeated presidential candidate Getúlio Vargas, supported by the majority of military,[96] lead a coup d'état and assume the presidency.[97]

The Brazilian coup d'état of 1930 raised Getúlio Vargas (center with military uniform but no hat) to power. He ruled the country for fifteen years.

Vargas and the military, who were supposed to assume the government temporarily to implement democratic reforms related to 1891's Constitution, closed the Congress and ruled with emergency powers, replacing the states' governors with their supporters.[98] [99] Under the Claiming of the broken promises of changing, in 1932 the oligarchy of São Paulo tried to regain the power[100] and in 1935 the Communists rebelled,[101] having both been defeated. However, the communist threat served as an excuse for Vargas to preclude elections launching another coup d'état in 1937, creating a full dictatorship[102] [103] [104] [105] In May 1938, there was another failed attempt to take over the power by local fascists.[106] [107]

In foreign policy, the success in resolving border disputes with neighboring countries[108] in the early years of this period, was followed by a failed attempt to permanently exert a prominent role in the League of Nations[109] after military involvement in World War I.[110] [111] [112] Notwithstanding, Brazil remained neutral at the beginning of World War II until the Pan-American Conference of January 1942 when Brazil stood alongside the U.S.A. severing diplomatic relations with the Axis powers.[113] In retaliation, Nazi Germany and Fascist Italy extended their submarine warfare against Brazil, which led the country to enter the war on the allied side in August of that year.[114] [115]

With the allied victory in 1945 and the end of the Nazi-fascist regimes in Europe, Vargas's position became unsustainable and he was swiftly overthrown in another military coup.[116] Democracy was reinstated and General Eurico Gaspar Dutra was elected president taking office in 1946.[117] Having returned to power democratically elected at the end of 1950, Vargas committed suicide in August 1954 amid a political crisis.[118] [119]

Contemporary era

Several brief interim governments succeeded after Vargas's suicide.[120] Juscelino Kubitscheck became president in 1956 and assumed a conciliatory posture towards the political opposition that allowed him to govern without major crises.[121] The economy and industrial sector grew remarkably,[122] but his greatest achievement was the construction of the new capital city of Brasília, inaugurated in 1960.[123] His successor was Jânio Quadros, who resigned in 1961 less than a year after taking office.[124] His vice-president, João Goulart, assumed the presidency, but aroused strong political opposition[125] and was deposed in April 1964 by a coup that resulted in a military regime.[126]

The transition from Fernando Henrique Cardoso to Luís Inácio Lula da Silva indicated that Brazil had finally succeeded in achieving its long-sought political stability.

The new regime was intended to be transitory[127] but it gradually closed in on itself and became a full dictatorship with the promulgation of the Fifth Institutional Act in 1968.[128] The repression of the dictatorship's opponents, including urban guerrillas,[129] was harsh, but not as brutal as in other Latin American countries.[130] Due to the extraordinary economic growth, known as an "economic miracle", the regime reached its highest level of popularity in the years of repression.[131]

General Ernesto Geisel became president in 1974 and began his project of re-democratization through a process that he said would be "slow, gradual and safe."[132] [133] Geisel ended the military indiscipline that had plagued the country since 1889,[134] as well as the torture of political prisoners, censorship of the press,[135] and finally, the dictatorship itself, after he extinguished the Fifth Institutional Act.[128] However, the military regime continued, under his chosen successor General João Figueiredo, to complete the transition to full democracy.[136]

The civilians fully returned to power in 1985 when José Sarney assumed the presidency[137] but, by the end of his term, he had become extremely unpopular due to the uncontrollable economic crisis and unusually high inflation.[138] Sarney's unsuccessful government allowed the election in 1989 of the almost unknown Fernando Collor, who was subsequently impeached by the National Congress in 1992.[139] Collor was succeeded by his Vice-President Itamar Franco, who appointed Fernando Henrique Cardoso as Minister of Finance. Cardoso produced a highly successful Plano Real (Royal or Real Plan)[140] that granted stability to the Brazilian economy[141] and he was elected as president in 1994 and again in 1998.[142] The peaceful transition of power to Luís Inácio Lula da Silva, who was elected in 2002 and re-elected in 2006, proved that Brazil had finally succeeded in achieving its long-sought political stability.[143] Lula was succeeded in 2011 by the current president, Dilma Rousseff.[144]

Geography

Brazil occupies a large area along the eastern coast of South America and includes much of the continent's interior,[145] sharing land borders with Uruguay to the south; Argentina and Paraguay to the southwest; Bolivia and Peru to the west; Colombia to the northwest; and Venezuela, Suriname, Guyana and the French overseas department of French Guiana to the north. It shares a border with every country in South America except for Ecuador and Chile. It also encompasses a number of oceanic archipelagos, such as Fernando de Noronha, Rocas Atoll, Saint Peter and Paul Rocks, and Trindade and Martim Vaz.[12] Its size, relief, climate, and natural resources make Brazil geographically diverse.[145] Including its Atlantic islands, Brazil lies between latitudes 6°N and 34°S, and longitudes 28° and 74°W.

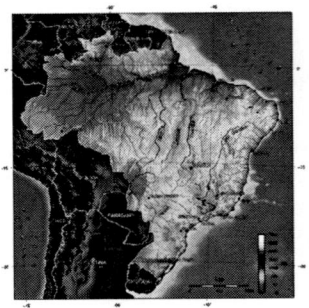

Topography map of Brazil

Brazil is the fifth largest country in the world, after Russia, Canada, China and the United States, and third largest in the Americas; with a total area of 8514876.599 km^2 (sq mi),[146] including 55455 km^2 (21411 sq mi) of water.[12] It spans three time zones; from UTC-4 in the western states, to UTC-3 in the eastern states (and the official time of Brazil) and UTC-2 in the Atlantic islands.[9] Brazil is the only country in the world that lies on the equator while having contiguous territory outside the tropics.

Brazilian topography is also diverse and includes hills, mountains, plains, highlands, and scrublands. Much of the terrain lies between 200 metres (660 ft) and 800 metres (2600 ft) in elevation.[147] The main upland area occupies most of the southern half of the country.[147] The northwestern parts of the plateau consist of broad, rolling terrain broken by low, rounded hills.[147]

The southeastern section is more rugged, with a complex mass of ridges and mountain ranges reaching elevations of up to 1200 metres (3900 ft).[147] These ranges include the Mantiqueira and Espinhaço mountains and the Serra do

Mar.[147] In the north, the Guiana Highlands form a major drainage divide, separating rivers that flow south into the Amazon Basin from rivers that empty into the Orinoco River system, in Venezuela, to the north. The highest point in Brazil is the Pico da Neblina at 2994 metres (9823 ft), and the lowest is the Atlantic Ocean.[12]

Brazil has a dense and complex system of rivers, one of the world's most extensive, with eight major drainage basins, all of which drain into the Atlantic.[148] Major rivers include the Amazon (the world's second-longest river and the largest in terms of volume of water), the Paraná and its major tributary the Iguaçu (which includes the Iguazu Falls), the Negro, São Francisco, Xingu, Madeira and Tapajós rivers.[148]

Climate

Snow in São Joaquim, Santa Catarina in 2010 (South) and tropical climate in Boa Viagem, Recife, Pernambuco (Northeast).

The climate of Brazil comprises a wide range of weather conditions across a large area and varied topography, but most of the country is tropical.[12] According to the Köppen system, Brazil hosts five major climatic subtypes: equatorial, tropical, semiarid, highland tropical, temperate, and subtropical. The different climatic conditions produce environments ranging from equatorial rainforests in the north and semiarid deserts in the northeast, to temperate coniferous forests in the south and tropical savannas in central Brazil.[149] Many regions have starkly different microclimates.[150][151]

An equatorial climate characterizes much of northern Brazil. There is no real dry season, but there are some variations in the period of the year when most rain falls.[149] Temperatures average 25 °C (77 °F),[151] with more significant temperature variation between night and day than between seasons.[150]

Over central Brazil rainfall is more seasonal, characteristic of a savanna climate.[150] This region is as extensive as the Amazon basin but has a very different climate as it lies farther south at a higher altitude.[149] In the interior northeast, seasonal rainfall is even more extreme. The semiarid climatic region generally receives less than 800 millimetres (31.5 in) of rain,[152] most of which generally falls in a period of three to five months of the year[153] and occasionally less than this, creating long periods of drought.[150] Brazil's 1877–78 *Grande Seca* (Great Drought), the most severe ever recorded in Brazil,[154] caused approximately half a million deaths.[155] The one from 1915 was devastating too.[156]

South of Bahia, near São Paulo, the distribution of rainfall changes, with rain falling throughout the year.[149] The south enjoys temperate conditions, with cool winters and average annual temperatures not exceeding 18 °C (64.4 °F);[151] winter frosts are quite common, with occasional snowfall in the higher areas.[149][150]

Biodiversity

Brazil's large territory comprises different ecosystems, such as the Amazon Rainforest, recognized as having the greatest biological diversity in the world,[157] with the Atlantic Forest and the Cerrado, sustaining the greatest biodiversity.[158] In the south, the Araucaria pine forest grows under temperate conditions.[158]

The rich wildlife of Brazil reflects the variety of natural habitats. Scientists estimate that the total number of plant and animal species in Brazil could approach four million.[158]

Larger mammals include pumas, jaguars, ocelots, rare bush dogs, and foxes; peccaries, tapirs, anteaters, sloths, opossums, and armadillos are abundant. Deer are plentiful in the south, and many species of New World monkeys are found in the northern rain forests.[158] [159] Concern for the environment has grown in response to global interest in environmental issues.[160]

The Amazon Rainforest, the largest tropical forest in the world.

Environment

The natural heritage of Brazil is severely threatened by cattle ranching and agriculture, logging, mining, resettlement, oil and gas extraction, over-fishing, wildlife trade, dams and infrastructure, water contamination, climate change, fire, and invasive species.[157] In many areas of the country, the natural environment is threatened by development.[161] Construction of highways has opened up previously remote areas for agriculture and settlement; dams have flooded valleys and inundated wildlife habitats; and mines have scarred and polluted the landscape.[160] [162] At least 70 dams are said to be planned for the Amazon region, including controversial Belo Monte hydroelectric dam.[163]

Politics

The Brazilian Federation is the "indissoluble union" of three distinct political entities: the States, the Municipalities and the Federal District.[15] The Union, the states and the Federal District, and the municipalities, are the "spheres of government." The Federation is set on five fundamental principles:[15] sovereignty, citizenship, dignity of human beings, the social values of labour and freedom of enterprise, and political pluralism. The classic tripartite branches of government (executive, legislative, and judicial under the checks and balances system), is formally established by the Constitution.[15] The executive and legislative are organized independently in all three spheres of government, while the judiciary is organized only at the federal and state/Federal District spheres.

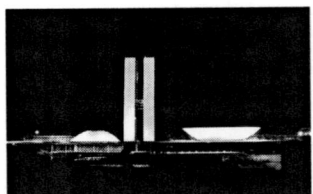

The National Congress in Brasília, the capital of Brazil.

All members of the executive and legislative branches are directly elected.[164] [165] [166] Judges and other judicial officials are appointed after passing entry exams.[164] Brazil has a multi-party system for most of its history. Voting is compulsory for the literate between 18 and 70 years old and optional for illiterates and those between 16 and 18 or beyond 70.[15] Together with several smaller parties, four political parties stand out: Workers' Party (PT), Brazilian Social Democracy Party (PSDB), Brazilian Democratic Movement Party (PMDB), and Democrats (DEM). Almost all governmental and administrative functions are exercised by authorities and agencies affiliated to the Executive.

The form of government is that of a democratic republic, with a presidential system.[15] The president is both head of state and head of government of the Union and is elected for a four-year term,[15] with the possibility of re-election for a second successive term. The current president is Dilma Rousseff who was inaugurated on January 1, 2011.[167] The President appoints the Ministers of State, who assist in government.[15] Legislative houses in each political entity are the main source of law in Brazil. The National Congress is the Federation's bicameral legislature, consisting of the Chamber of Deputies and the Federal Senate. Judiciary authorities exercise jurisdictional duties almost exclusively.

Fifteen political parties are represented in Congress. It is common for politicians to switch parties, and thus the proportion of congressional seats held by particular parties changes regularly. The largest political parties are the Workers' Party (PT), Democrats (DEM), Brazilian Democratic Movement Party (PMDB-center), Brazilian Social Democratic Party (PSDB), Progressive Party (PP), Brazilian Labor Party (PTB), Liberal Party (PL), Brazilian Socialist Party (PSB), Popular Socialist Party (PPS), Democratic Labor Party (PDT), and the Communist Party of Brazil (PCdoB).[168]

Law

Brazilian law is based on Roman-Germanic traditions[169] and civil law concepts prevail over common law practice. Most of Brazilian law is codified, although non-codified statutes also represent a substantial part, playing a complementary role. Court decisions set out interpretive guidelines; however, they are seldom binding on other specific cases. Doctrinal works and the works of academic jurists have strong influence in law creation and in law cases.

Supreme Federal Court building at the Three Powers Plaza.

The legal system is based on the Federal Constitution, which was promulgated on 5 October 1988, and is the fundamental law of Brazil. All other legislation and court decisions must conform to its rules.[170]

As of April 2007, there have been 53 amendments. States have their own constitutions, which must not contradict the Federal Constitution.[171] Municipalities and the Federal District have "organic laws" (*leis orgânicas*), which act in a similar way to constitutions.[15] [172] Legislative entities are the main source of statutes, although in certain matters judiciary and executive bodies may enact legal norms.[15] Jurisdiction is administered by the judiciary entities, although in rare situations the Federal Constitution allows the Federal Senate to pass on legal judgments.[15] There are also specialized military, labor, and electoral courts.[15] The highest court is the Supreme Federal Court.

This system has been criticised over the last few decades for the slow pace of decision making. Lawsuits on appeal may take several years to resolve, and in some cases more than a decade elapses before definitive rulings.[173] Nevertheless, the Supreme Federal Tribunal was the first court in the world to transmit its sessions on television, and also via YouTube.[174] [175] More recently, in December 2009, the Supreme Court adopted Twitter to display items on the day planner of the ministers, to inform the daily actions of the Court and the most important decisions made by them.[176]

Brazil continues to have high crime rates in a number of statistics, despite recent improvements. More than 500,000 people have been killed by firearms in Brazil between 1979 and 2003, according to a new report by the United Nations.[177] In 2010, there were 473,600 people incarcerated in Brazilian prisons and jails.[178]

Foreign relations

Brazil is a political and economic leader in Latin America.[179] [180] However, social and economic problems have prevented it from becoming an effective global power.[181] Between 1945 and 1990, both democratic and military governments sought to expand Brazil's influence in the world by pursuing a state-led industrial policy and an independent foreign policy. More recently, the country has aimed to strengthen ties with other South American countries, and engage in multilateral diplomacy through the United Nations and the Organization of American States.[182]

Itamaraty Palace, headquarters of the Ministry of Foreign Affairs.

Brazil's current foreign policy is based on the country's position as a regional power in Latin America, a leader among developing countries, and an emerging world power.[183] In general, current Brazilian foreign policy reflects multilateralism, peaceful dispute settlement, and nonintervention in the affairs of other countries.[184] The Brazilian Constitution also determines that the country shall seek the economic, political, social and cultural integration of the nations of Latin America.[15] [185] [186] [187]

An increasingly well-developed tool of Brazil's foreign policy is providing aid as a donor to other developing countries.[188] Brazil does not just use its growing economic strength to provide financial aid, but it also provides high levels of expertise and most importantly of all, a quiet non-confrontational diplomacy to improve governance levels.[188] Total aid is estimated to be around $1 billion per year that includes:[188]

- technical cooperation of around $480 million ($30 million in 2010 provided directly by the Brazilian Cooperation Agency (ABC))
- an estimated $450 million for in-kind expertise provided by Brazilian institutions specialising in technical cooperation

In addition, Brazil manages a peacekeeping mission in Haiti ($350 million) and makes in-kind contributions to the World Food Programme ($300 million).[188] This is in addition to humanitarian assistance and contributions to multilateral development agencies. The scale of this aid places it on par with China and India and ahead of many western donors.[188] The Brazilian South-South aid has been described as a "global model in waiting."[189]

Military

The armed forces of Brazil consist of the Brazilian Army, the Brazilian Navy, and the Brazilian Air Force. With a total of 371,199 active personnel,[190] they comprise the largest armed force in Latin America.[191] The Army is responsible for land-based military operations and has 235,978 active personnel.[192]

The Military Police (States' Military Police) is described as an ancillary force of the Army by the constitution, but is under the control of each state's governor.[15] The Navy is responsible for naval operations and for guarding Brazilian territorial waters. It is the oldest of the Brazilian armed forces and the only navy in Latin America to operate an aircraft carrier, the NAe São Paulo (formerly FS *Foch* of the French Navy).[193] The Air Force is the aerial warfare branch of the Brazilian armed forces, and the largest air force in Latin America, with about 700 manned aircraft in service.[194]

Administrative divisions

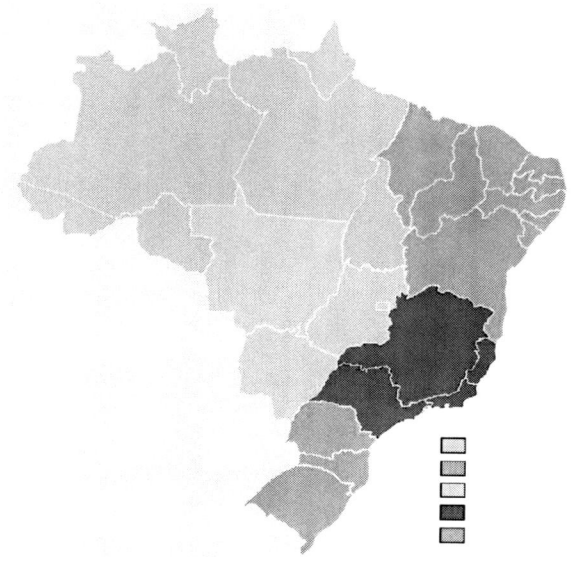

Atlantic Ocean

Pacific Ocean

North Region

Northeast Region

Central-West Region

Southeast Region

South Region

Acre

Amazonas

Pará

Roraima

Amapá

Rondônia

Tocantins

Maranhão

Bahia

Piauí

Ceará

Rio Grande do Norte

Paraíba

Pernambuco

Alagoas

Sergipe

Mato Grosso

Mato Grosso do Sul

Federal District

Goiás

Minas Gerais

São Paulo

Rio de Janeiro

Espírito Santo

Paraná

Santa Catarina

Rio Grande do Sul

Argentina

Bolivia

Chile

Colombia

French Guiana

Guyana

Paraguay

Peru

Suriname

Uruguay

Venezuela

Brazil is a federation composed of 26 States, one federal district (which contains the capital city, Brasília) and municipalities.[15] States have autonomous administrations, collect their own taxes and receive a share of taxes collected by the Federal government. They have a governor and a unicameral legislative body elected directly by their voters. They also have independent Courts of Law for common justice. Despite this, states have much less autonomy to create their own laws than in the United States. For example, criminal and civil laws can only be voted by the federal bicameral Congress and are uniform throughout the country.[15]

The states and the federal district may be grouped into regions: Northern, Northeast, Central-West, Southeast and Southern. The Brazilian regions are merely geographical, not political or administrative divisions, and they do not have any specific form of government. Although defined by law, Brazilian regions are useful mainly for statistical purposes, and also to define the application of federal funds in development projects.

Municipalities, as the states, have autonomous administrations, collect their own taxes and receive a share of taxes collected by the Union and state government.[15] Each has a mayor and an elected legislative body, but no separate Court of Law. Indeed, a Court of Law organized by the state can encompass many municipalities in a single justice administrative division called *comarca* (county).

Economy

An Embraer ERJ-135 commercial jet. Brazil is the world's third largest aircraft producer.

Brazil is the largest national economy in Latin America, the world's seventh largest economy at market exchange rates and the eighth largest in purchasing power parity (PPP), according to the International Monetary Fund and the World Bank. Brazil has a mixed economy with abundant natural resources. The Brazilian economy has been predicted to become one of the five largest in the world in the decades to come, the GDP per capita following and growing.[195] Its current GDP (PPP) per capita is $10,200, putting Brazil in the 64th position according to World Bank data. It has large and developed agricultural, mining, manufacturing and service sectors, as well as a large labor pool.[196]

Brazilian exports are booming, creating a new generation of tycoons.[197] Major export products include aircraft, electrical equipment, automobiles, ethanol, textiles, footwear, iron ore, steel, coffee, orange juice, soybeans and corned beef.[198] The country has been expanding its presence in international financial and commodities markets, and is one of a group of four emerging economies called the BRIC countries.[199]

Brazil pegged its currency, the real, to the U.S. dollar in 1994. However, after the East Asian financial crisis, the Russian default in 1998[200] and the series of adverse financial events that followed it, the Central Bank of Brazil temporarily changed its monetary policy to a managed-float scheme while undergoing a currency crisis, until definitively changing the exchange regime to free-float in January 1999.[201]

Brazil received an International Monetary Fund rescue package in mid-2002 of $30.4 billion,[203] then a record sum. Brazil's central bank paid back the IMF loan in 2005, although it was not due to be repaid until 2006.[204] One of the issues the Central Bank of Brazil recently dealt with was an excess of speculative short-term capital inflows to the country, which may have contributed to a fall in the value of the U.S. dollar against the real during that period.[205] Nonetheless, foreign direct investment (FDI), related to long-term, less speculative investment in production, is estimated to be $193.8 billion for 2007.[206] Inflation monitoring and control currently plays a major part in the Central bank's role of setting out short-term interest rates as a monetary policy measure.[207]

Combine in a cotton Brazilian plantation. Brazil is the third largest exporter of agricultural products in the world.[202]

Between 1993 and 2010, 7'012 mergers & acquisitions with a total known value of $707 billion with the involvement of Brazlian firms have been announced.[208] The year 2010 was a new record in terms of value with 115 bil. USD of transactions. The largest transaction with involvement of Brazilian companies has been: Cia Vale do Rio Doce acquired Inco in a tender offer valued at $18.9 billion USD.

The purchasing power in Brazil is eroded by the so-called Brazil cost.[209]

Components and energy

Itaipu Dam, the world's largest hydroelectric plant by energy generation and second-largest by installed capacity.

Brazil's economy is diverse,[210] encompassing agriculture, industry, and many services.[197] [211] [212] [213] The recent economic strength has been due in part to a global boom in commodities prices with exports from beef to soybeans soaring.[212] [213] Agriculture and allied sectors like forestry, logging and fishing accounted for 5.1% of the gross domestic product in 2007,[214] a performance that puts agribusiness in a position of distinction in terms of Brazil's trade balance, in spite of trade barriers and subsidizing policies adopted by the developed countries.[215] [216]

The industry — from automobiles, steel and petrochemicals to computers, aircraft, and consumer durables— accounted for 30.8% of the gross domestic product.[214] Industry, which is often technologically advanced, is highly concentrated in metropolitan São Paulo, Rio de Janeiro, Campinas, Porto Alegre, and Belo Horizonte.[217]

Brazil is the world's tenth largest energy consumer with much of its energy coming from renewable sources, particularly hydroelectricity and ethanol; nonrenewable energy is mainly produced from oil and natural gas.[218] A global power in agriculture and natural resources, Brazil experienced tremendous economic growth over the past three decades.[219] It is expected to become a major oil producer and exporter, having recently made huge oil discoveries.[220] [221] [222] The governmental agencies responsible for the energy policy are the Ministry of Mines and Energy, the National Council for Energy Policy, the National Agency of Petroleum, Natural Gas and Biofuels, and the National Agency of Electricity.[223] [224]

Science and technology

Technological research in Brazil is largely carried out in public universities and research institutes. But more than 73% of funding for basic research still comes from government sources.[225] Some of Brazil's most notable technological hubs are the Oswaldo Cruz Institute, the Butantan Institute, the Air Force's Aerospace Technical Center, the Brazilian Agricultural Research Corporation and the INPE. The Brazilian Space Agency has the most advanced space program in Latin America, with significant capabilities in launch vehicles, launch sites and satellite manufacturing.[226]

Brazilian National Laboratory of Synchrotron Light in Campinas.

Uranium is enriched at the Resende Nuclear Fuel Factory to fuel the country's energy demands and plans are underway to build the country's first nuclear submarine.[227] Brazil is one of the three countries in Latin America[228] with an operational Synchrotron Laboratory, a research facility on physics, chemistry, material science and life sciences. And Brazil is the first and only Latin American country to have a semiconductor company with its own fab, the CEITEC.[229]

Transport

Brazil has a large and diverse transport network. Roads are the primary carriers of freight and passenger traffic. The road system totaled 1.98 million km (1.23 million mi) in 2002. The total of paved roads increased from 35,496 km (22,056 mi) in 1967 to 184,140 km (114,425 mi) in 2002.[230]

BR-116 highway in the outskirts of Fortaleza.

Recife Airport

Brazil's railway system has been declining since 1945, when emphasis shifted to highway construction. The total length of railway track was 30,875 km (19,186 mi) in 2002, as compared with 31,848 km (19,789 mi) in 1970. Most of the railway system belongs to the Federal Railroad Corp., with a majority government interest. The government also privatized seven lines in 1997.[231] The São Paulo Metro was the first underground transit system in Brazil. The other metro systems are in Rio de Janeiro, Porto Alegre, Recife, Belo Horizonte, Brasília, Teresina, Fortaleza, and Salvador.

There are about 2,500 airports in Brazil, including landing fields: the second largest number in the world, after the United States.[232] São Paulo-Guarulhos International Airport, near São Paulo, is the largest and busiest airport, handling the vast majority of popular and commercial traffic of the country and connecting the city with virtually all major cities across the world.[233]

Coastal shipping links widely separated parts of the country. Bolivia and Paraguay have been given free ports at Santos. Of the 36 deep-water ports, Santos, Itajaí, Rio Grande, Paranaguá, Rio de Janeiro, Sepetiba, Vitória, Suape, Manaus and São Francisco do Sul are some of the most important.[234]

Demographics

Race and ethnicity in Brazil[235] [236] [237]	
Ethnicity	Percentage
White	47.3%
Brown (Multiracial)	43.1%
Black	7.6%
Asian	2.1%
Amerindian	0.3%

The population of Brazil, as recorded by the 2008 PNAD, was approximately 190 million[238] (22.31 inhabitants per square kilometer), with a ratio of men to women of 0.95:1[239] and 83.75% of the population defined as urban.[240] The population is heavily concentrated in the Southeastern (79.8 million inhabitants) and Northeastern (53.5 million inhabitants) regions, while the two most extensive regions, the Center-West and the North, which together make up

64.12% of the Brazilian territory, have a total of only 29.1 million inhabitants.

The first census in Brazil was carried out in 1872 and recorded a population of 9,930,478.[241] From 1880 to 1930, 4 million Europeans arrived.[242] Brazil's population increased significantly between 1940 and 1970, due to a decline in the mortality rate, even though the birth rate underwent a slight decline. In the 1940s the annual population growth rate was 2.4%, rising to 3.0% in the 1950s and remaining at 2.9% in the 1960s, as life expectancy rose from 44 to 54 years[243] and to 72.6 years in 2007.[244] It has been steadily falling since the 1960s, from 3.04% per year between 1950–1960 to 1.05% in 2008 and is expected to fall to a negative value of −0.29% by 2050 [245] thus completing the demographic transition.[246]

Brazilians of Italian descent with former President of Brazil, in Rio Grande do Sul.

According to the National Research by Household Sample (PNAD) of 2008, 48.43% of the population (about 92 million) described themselves as White; 43.80% (about 83 million) as Brown (Multiracial), 6.84% (about 13 million) as Black; 0.58% (about 1.1 million) as Asian; and 0.28% (about 536 thousand) as Amerindian, while 0.07% (about 130 thousand) did not declare their race.[247]

In 2007, the National Indian Foundation reported the existence of 67 different uncontacted tribes, up from 40 in 2005. Brazil is believed to have the largest number of uncontacted peoples in the world.[248]

About 85% to 95% of Brazilians descend from the country's indigenous peoples, Portuguese settlers, and African slaves.[249] Since the arrival of the Portuguese in 1500, considerable intermarriage between these three groups has taken place. The brown population (as multiracial Brazilians are officially called; *pardo* in Portuguese, also colloquially *moreno*, or swarthy)[250] [251] is a broad category that includes Caboclos (descendants of Whites and Indians), Mulattoes (descendants of Whites and Blacks) and Cafuzos (descendants of Blacks and Indians).[249] [250] [251] [252] [253] [254] Caboclos form the majority of the population in the Northern, Northeastern and Central-Western regions.[255] A large Mulatto population can be found in the eastern coast of the northeastern region from Bahia to Paraíba[254] [256] and also in northern Maranhão,[257] [258] southern Minas Gerais[259] and in eastern Rio de Janeiro.[254] [259] From the 19th century, Brazil opened its borders to immigration. About five million people from over 60 countries migrated to Brazil between 1808 and 1972, most of them from Portugal, Italy, Spain, Germany, Japan and the Middle-East.[260]

In 2008, the illiteracy rate was 11.48%[261] and among the youth (ages 15–19) 1.74%. It was highest (20.30%) in the Northeast, which had a large proportion of rural poor.[262] Illiteracy was high (24.18%) among the rural population and lower (9.05%) among the urban population.[263]

Religion

Religion in Brazil (2000 Census)[264]	
Religion	Percent
Roman Catholicism	73.8%
Protestantism	15.4%
No religion	7.4%
Spiritism	1.3%
Others	2.1%

Brazil possesses a richly spiritual society formed from the meeting of the Roman Catholic Church with the religious traditions of African slaves and indigenous peoples. This confluence of faiths during the Portuguese colonization of Brazil led to the development of a diverse array of syncretistic practices within the overarching umbrella of Brazilian

Roman Catholicism, characterized by traditional Portuguese festivities.[265] Religious pluralism increased during the 20th century, largely due to a Protestant community that has grown to include over 15% of the population.

Roman Catholicism is the country's predominant faith. Brazil has the world's largest Catholic population.[266] According to the 2000 Demographic Census (the PNAD survey does not inquire about religion), 73.57% of the population followed Roman Catholicism; 15.41% Protestantism; 1.33% Kardecist spiritism; 1.22% other Christian denominations; 0.31% Afro-Brazilian religions; 0.13% Buddhism; 0.05% Judaism; 0.02% Islam; 0.01% Amerindian religions; 0.59% other religions, undeclared or undetermined; while 7.35% have no religion.[264]

However, in the last ten years Protestantism, particularly Pentecostal Protestantism, has spread in Brazil, while the proportion of Catholics has dropped significantly.[267] After Protestantism, individuals professing no religion are also a significant group, exceeding 7% of the population in the 2000 census. The cities of Boa Vista, Salvador and Porto Velho have the greatest proportion of irreligious residents in Brazil. Teresina, Fortaleza, and Florianópolis were the most catholic of the country.[268]

Urbanization

According to IBGE (Brazilian Institute of Geography and Statistics) urban areas already concentrate 84.35% of the population, while the Southeast region remains the most populated one, with over 80 million inhabitants.[269] The largest metropolitan areas in Brazil are São Paulo, Rio de Janeiro, and Belo Horizonte — all in the Southeastern Region — with 19.5, 11.5, and 5.1 million inhabitants respectively.[270] Almost all of the state capitals are the largest cities in their states, except for Vitória, the capital of Espírito Santo, and Florianópolis, the capital of Santa Catarina. There are also non-capital metropolitan areas in the states of São Paulo (Campinas, Santos and the Paraíba Valley), Minas Gerais (Steel Valley), Rio Grande do Sul (Sinos Valley), and Santa Catarina (Itajaí Valley).[271]

Language

Museum of the Portuguese Language in São Paulo, the first language museum in the world.

The official language of Brazil is Portuguese,[13] which almost all of the population speaks and is virtually the only language used in newspapers, radio, television, and for business and administrative purposes. The exception to this is in the municipality of São Gabriel da Cachoeira where Nheengatu, a currently endangered South American creole language with mostly Indigenous Brazilian languages lexicon and Portuguese-based grammar that once was a major lingua franca in Brazil, has been granted co-official status with Portuguese.[272] Brazil is the only Portuguese-speaking nation in the Americas, making the language an important part of Brazilian national identity and giving it a national culture distinct from those of its Spanish-speaking neighbors.[273]

Brazilian Portuguese has had its own development, mostly similar to 16th century Central and Southern dialects of European Portuguese[274] (despite a very substantial number of Portuguese colonial settlers, and more recent immigrants, coming from Northern regions, and in minor degree Portuguese Macaronesia), with some influences from the Amerindian and African languages, especially West African and Bantu.[275] As a result, the language is somewhat different, mostly in phonology, from the language of Portugal and other Portuguese-speaking countries (the dialects of the other countries, partly due to the more recent end of Portuguese colonialism in these regions, have a closer connexion to contemporary European Portuguese). These differences are comparable to those between American and British English.[275]

In 1990, the Community of Portuguese Language Countries (CPLP), which included representatives from all countries with Portuguese as the official language, reached an agreement on the reform of the Portuguese orthography to unify the two standards then in use by Brazil on one side and the remaining lusophone countries on the other. This spelling reform went into effect in Brazil on January 1, 2009. In Portugal, the reform was signed into law by the President on July 21, 2008 allowing for a 6-year adaptation period, during which both orthographies will co-exist. The remaining CPLP countries are free to establish their own transition chronogram.[276]

Minority languages are spoken throughout the nation. One hundred and eighty Amerindian languages are spoken in remote areas and a number of other languages are spoken by immigrants and their descendants.[275] There are significant communities of German (mostly the Hunsrückisch, a High German language dialect) and Italian (mostly the Talian dialect, of Venetian origin) speakers in the south of the country, both of which are influenced by the Portuguese language.[277] [278] Brazil is the first country in South America to offer Esperanto to High School students.[279]

Culture

The core culture of Brazil is derived from Portuguese culture, because of its strong colonial ties with the Portuguese empire. Among other influences, the Portuguese introduced the Portuguese language, Roman Catholicism and colonial architectural styles.[280] The culture was, however, also strongly influenced by African, indigenous and non-Portuguese European cultures and traditions.[281] Some aspects of Brazilian culture were influenced by the contributions of Italian, German and other European immigrants who arrived in large numbers in the South and Southeast of Brazil.[282] The indigenous Amerindians influenced Brazil's language and cuisine; and the Africans influenced language, cuisine, music, dance and religion.[283]

Brazilian art has developed since the 16th century into different styles that range from Baroque (the dominant style in Brazil until the early 19th century)[285] [286] to Romanticism, Modernism, Expressionism, Cubism, Surrealism and Abstractionism.

Brazilian cinema dates back to the birth of the medium in the late 19th century and has gained a new level of international acclaim in recent years.[287]

Machado de Assis, poet and novelist whose work extends to almost all literary genres, is widely regarded as the greatest Brazilian writer.[284]

Music

Brazilian music encompasses various regional styles influenced by African, European and Amerindian forms. It developed distinctive styles, among them samba, MPB, choro, Sertanejo, brega, forró, frevo, maracatu, bossa nova, and axé.

Literature

Brazilian literature dates back to the 16th century, to the writings of the first Portuguese explorers in Brazil, such as Pêro Vaz de Caminha, filled with descriptions of fauna, flora and natives that amazed Europeans that arrived in Brazil.[288] Brazil produced significant works in Romanticism — novelists like Joaquim Manuel de Macedo and José de Alencar wrote novels about love and pain. Alencar, in his long career, also treated Indigenous people as heroes in the Indigenist novels *O Guarany, Iracema, Ubirajara*.[289]

Cuisine

Feijoada, a dish made with black beans, pork, rice, collard greens, cassava flour and orange

Brazilian cuisine varies greatly by region, reflecting the country's mix of native and immigrant populations. This has created a national cuisine marked by the preservation of regional differences.[290] Examples are Feijoada, considered the country's national dish;[291] and regional foods such as vatapá, moqueca, polenta and acarajé.[292]

Brazil has a variety of candies such as brigadeiros (chocolate fudge balls), cocada (a coconut sweet), beijinhos (coconut truffles and clove) and romeu e julieta (cheese with a guava jam known as goiabada). Peanut is used to make paçoca, rapadura and pé-de-moleque. Local common fruits like açaí, cupuaçu, mango, papaya, cocoa, cashew, guava, orange, passionfruit, pineapple, and hog plum are turned in juices and used to make chocolates, popsicles and ice cream.[293]

Popular snacks are pastel (a pastry), coxinha (chicken croquete), pão de queijo (cheese bread and cassava flour / tapioca), pamonha (corn and milk paste), esfirra (Lebanese pastry), kibbeh (from Arabic cuisine), empanada (pastry) and empada little salt pies filled with shrimps or hearth of palm.

But the everyday meal consist mosty of rice and beans with beef and salad.[294] Its common to mix it with cassava flour (farofa). Fried potatoes, fried cassava, fried banana, fried meat and fried cheese are very often eaten in lunch and served in most typical restaurants.[295]

The national beverage is coffee and cachaça is Brazil's native liquor. Cachaça is distilled from sugar cane and is the main ingredient in the national cocktail, Caipirinha.

Sports

The most popular sport in Brazil is football (soccer). The Brazilian national football team is ranked among the best in the world according to the FIFA World Rankings, and has won the World Cup tournament a record five times.[297] Basketball, volleyball, auto racing, and martial arts also attract large audiences. Brazil men's national volleyball team, for example, currently holds the titles of the World League, World Grand Champions Cup, World Championship and the World Cup. Others sports practiced in Brazil are tennis, team handball, swimming, and gymnastics have found a growing number of enthusiasts over the last decades. Some sport variations have their origins in Brazil: beach football,[298] futsal (indoor football)[299] and footvolley emerged in Brazil as variations of football. In martial arts, Brazilians developed Capoeira,[300] Vale tudo,[301] and Brazilian Jiu-Jitsu.[302] In auto racing, three Brazilian drivers have won the Formula One world championship eight times.[303] [304] [305]

Football (soccer) is the most popular sport in Brazil.[296]

Brazil has hosted several high-profile international sporting events, including UFC 134, the 1950 FIFA World Cup[306] and has been chosen to host the 2014 FIFA World Cup.[307] The São Paulo circuit, Autódromo José Carlos Pace, hosts the annual Grand Prix of Brazil.[308] São Paulo organized the IV Pan American Games in 1963,[309] and Rio de Janeiro hosted the XV Pan American Games in 2007.[309] On 2 October 2009, Rio de Janeiro was selected to host the 2016 Olympic Games, the first to be held in South America[310] and second in Latin America after Mexico.

In May 2010 Brazil launched TV Brasil Internacional, an international television station, initially broadcasting to 49 countries. Luiz Inácio Lula da Silva, former President of Brazil, described its aim as "presenting Brazil to the

Brazil 79

world."[311]

See also
- International rankings of Brazil
- List of Brazilians

References
[1] "Demographics" (http://www.brasil.gov.br/sobre/brazil/brazil-in-numbers/demographics). Brazilian Government. 2011. . Retrieved 2011-10-08. (**English**)
[2] Caracteristicas da População e dos Domicílios do Censo Demográfico 2010 — Cor ou raça (http://www.ibge.gov.br/home/estatistica/populacao/censo2010/caracteristicas_da_populacao/tabelas_pdf/tab3.pdf)
[3] IBGE. 2011 Population Projection (http://www.ibge.gov.br/home/presidencia/noticias/noticia_impressao.php?id_noticia=1961)
[4] IBGE. Censo 2010: população do Brasil é de 190.732.694 pessoas (http://www.ibge.gov.br/home/presidencia/noticias/noticia_visualiza.php?id_noticia=1766&id_pagina=1).
[5] "Brazil" (http://www.imf.org/external/pubs/ft/weo/2011/01/weodata/weorept.aspx?sy=2008&ey=2011&scsm=1&ssd=1&sort=country&ds=.&br=1&c=223&s=NGDPD,NGDPDPC,PPPGDP,PPPPC,LP&grp=0&a=&pr.x=25&pr.y=4). International Monetary Fund. . Retrieved 2011-04-21.
[6] IMF 2011 GDP projections (http://www.imf.org/external/pubs/ft/weo/2011/02/weodata/weorept.aspx?sy=2011&ey=2011&scsm=1&ssd=1&sort=country&ds=.&br=1&c=512,941,914,446,612,666,614,668,311,672,213,946,911,137,193,962,122,674,912,676,313,548,419,556,513,678,316,181,913,682,124,684,339,273,638,&s=NGDPD&grp=0&a=&pr.x=22&pr.y=9)
[7] Caracteristicas da População e dos Domicílios do Censo Demográfico 2010 — Rendimento (http://www.ibge.gov.br/home/estatistica/populacao/censo2010/caracteristicas_da_populacao/tabelas_pdf/tab8.pdf)
[8] UNDP Human Development Report 2011. "Table 1: Human development index 2011 and its components" (http://hdr.undp.org/en/media/HDR_2011_EN_Table1.pdf) (PDF). UNDP. . Retrieved 2011-12-04.
[9] "Hora Legal Brasileira" (http://pcdsh01.on.br/Fusbr.htm). Observatório Nacional. . Retrieved 2009-02-21.
[10] As on for example the national website (http://www.brasil.gov.br/?set_language=en).
[11] Mugnier, Clifford (January 2009). *Grids & Datums – Federative Republic of Brazil* (http://www.asprs.org/resources/GRIDS/01-2009-brazil.pdf). .
[12] "Geography of Brazil" (https://www.cia.gov/library/publications/the-world-factbook/geos/br.html). Central Intelligence Agency. 2008. . Retrieved 2008-06-03.
[13] "People of Brazil" (https://www.cia.gov/library/publications/the-world-factbook/geos/br.html). Central Intelligence Agency. 2008. . Retrieved 2008-06-03.
[14] "Introduction of Brazil" (https://www.cia.gov/library/publications/the-world-factbook/geos/br.html). Central Intelligence Agency. 2008. . Retrieved 2008-06-03.
[15] "Brazilian Federal Constitution" (http://www.planalto.gov.br/ccivil_03/Constituicao/Constituiçao.htm) (in Portuguese). Presidency of the Republic. 1988. . Retrieved 2008-06-03. "Brazilian Federal Constitution" (http://www.v-brazil.com/government/laws/titleI.html). v-brazil.com. 2007. . Retrieved 2008-06-03. "Unofficial translate"
[16] "Territorial units of the municipality level" (http://www.sidra.ibge.gov.br/bda/territorio/tabunit.asp?n=6&t=2&z=t&o=4) (in Portuguese). Brazilian Institute of Geography and Statistics. 2008. . Retrieved 2008-06-03.
[17] " World Development Indicators database (http://siteresources.worldbank.org/DATASTATISTICS/Resources/GDP.pdf)" (PDF file). World Bank, 7 October 2009.
[18] "CIA – The World Factbook – Country Comparisons – GDP (purchasing power parity)" (https://www.cia.gov/library/publications/the-world-factbook/rankorder/2001rank.html). Cia.gov. . Retrieved 25 January 2011.
[19] Clendenning, Alan (2008-04-17). "Booming Brazil could be world power soon" (http://www.usatoday.com/money/economy/2008-04-17-310212789_x.htm). USA Today – The Associated Press. p. 2. . Retrieved 2008-12-12.
[20] CNRTL (http://www.cnrtl.fr/etymologie/brésil) – Centre National de Ressources Textuelles et Lexicales (**French**)
[21] Michaelis (http://michaelis.uol.com.br/moderno/portugues/index.php?lingua=portugues-portugues&palavra=brasil) – Moderno Dicionário da Língua Portuguesa (**Portuguese**)
[22] iDicionário Aulete (http://aulete.uol.com.br/site.php?mdl=aulete_digital&op=loadVerbete&pesquisa=1&palavra=brasil) (**Portuguese**)
[23] (**Portuguese**) Eduardo Bueno, *Brasil: uma História* (São Paulo: Ática, 2003; ISBN 8508082134), p.36.
[24] Boxer, p. 98.
[25] Boxer, p. 100.
[26] Boxer, pp. 100–101.
[27] Skidmore, p. 27.

[28] Boxer, p. 101.
[29] Boxer, p. 108
[30] Boxer, p. 102.
[31] Skidmore, pp. 30, 32.
[32] Skidmore, p. 36.
[33] Boxer, p. 110
[34] Skidmore, p. 34.
[35] Skidmore, pp. 32–33.
[36] Bueno, pp. 80–81.
[37] Facsimiles of multiple original documents (http://www.s4ulanguages.com/wic.html) relating about the events in Brazil in the 17th century that led to a Dutch influence and their final defeat
[38] Calmon, p. 294.
[39] Bueno, p. 86.
[40] Boxer, p. 164.
[41] Boxer, pp. 168, 170.
[42] Boxer, p. 169.
[43] Boxer, p. 207.
[44] Boxer, p. 213.
[45] Bueno, p. 145.
[46] Calmon (2002), p. 191.
[47] Lustosa, pp. 109–110
[48] Lustosa, pp. 117–119
[49] Lustosa, pp. 150–153
[50] Vianna, p. 418
[51] Hendrik Kraay *apud* Lorenzo Aldé, *Revista de História da Biblioteca Nacional,* issue 50, year 5 (Rio de Janeiro: SABIN, 2009), p. 20
[52] Sérgio Buarque de Holanda, *O Brasil Monárquico: o processo de emancipação,* 4th ed. (São Paulo: Difusão Européia do Livro, 1976), p. 403
[53] Diégues 2004, pp. 168, 164, 178
[54] Diégues 2004, pp. 179–180
[55] Lustosa, p. 208
[56] Vianna, p. 140
[57] José Murilo de Carvalho, *A Monarquia brasileira* (Rio de Janeiro: Ao Livro Técnico, 1993), p. 23
[58] Calmon (2002), p. 189
[59] Vainfas, p. 170
[60] Lyra (v.1), p. 17
[61] Carvalho 2007, p. 21
[62] Miriam Dohlnikoff, *Pacto imperial: origens do federalismo no Brasil do século XIX* (São Paulo: Globo, 2005), p. 206
[63] "A hora da desforra", por Júlio José Chiavenato, Revista História Viva, nº 45, páginas 84 a 91.
[64] Carvalho (2007), p. 43
[65] Souza, p. 326
[66] Janotti, pp. 171–172
[67] Munro, p. 273
[68] Barman (1999), pp.18, 27
[69] Lyra (v.1), pp. 164, 225, 272
[70] Carvalho (2007), pp. 9, 222
[71] Lyra (v.1), p. 166
[72] Lyra (v.3), p. 62
[73] Vainfas, p. 18
[74] Munro, p. 280
[75] George Ermakoff, *Rio de Janeiro – 1840–1900 – Uma crônica fotográfica* (Rio de Janeiro: G. Ermakoff Casa Editorial, 2006), p. 189
[76] Schwarcz, p. 444
[77] Vainfas, p. 201
[78] Barman (1999), p. 399
[79] Barman (1999), p. 130
[80] Lyra (v.3), p. 126
[81] Barman (1999), p. 361
[82] Ricardo Salles, *Nostalgia Imperial* (Rio de Janeiro: Topbooks, 1996), p. 194 – However, the monarchist reaction after the fall of the empire and the subsequent exile of the Imperial Family "was not small and even less was its repression".
[83] Lyra (v.3), p. 99

[84] Schwarcz, pp. 450, 457
[85] Richard W. Flournoy & Manley O. Hudson; "A Collection of nationality laws of various countries, as contained in Constitutions, Statutes and Treaties" Oxford University Press 1929 ISBN 0-8377-0544-4 Page 48
[86] Mortimer Sellers & Tadeusz Tomaszewski; "The Rule of Law in Comparative Perspective" Springer Science+Business Media BV 2010 Chapter 8.3.2, pages 113–117
[87] Herbert F. Wright; "The constitutions of the states at war 1914–1918" U.S. Govt. Print. Office 1919; in 1891's Brazilian constitution See article 43 § 4th and art.47
[88] Gail D. Triner; "Banking and economic development: Brazil, 1889–1930" Palgrave™ 2000 ISBN 0-312-23399-X Pages 44–74
[89] Levine; Robert M. "Vale of Tears: Revisiting the Canudos' Massacre in Northeastern Brazil, 1893–1897" University of California Press 1995 ISBN 0520203437 Pages 36–37; 55(last paragraph) and 330
[90] See Levine 1995, Chapter 4
[91] Sevcenko; Nicolau "A Revolta da Vacina" (**Portuguese**) Cosac Naify 2010 ISBN 9788575038680
[92] Barman, Roderick J. "Millenarian Vision, Capitalist Reality: Brazil's Contestado Rebellion, 1912–1916" Canadian Journal of History December 1, 1995 University of Saskatchewan Vol30 Nr3 Pg542
[93] E. Bradford Burns; "A History of Brazil" Columbia University Press 1993 ISBN 9780231079556 *from 2nd paragraph of p242 to p245*
[94] Roland, Maria Inês; "A Revolta da Chibata" (**Portuguese**) Saraiva 2000 ISBN 8502030957
[95] Woodward; James P. "A Place in Politics: São Paulo, Brazil, from Seigneurial Republicanism to Regionalist Revolt" Duke University Press Books 2009 ISBN 0822343290 Chapter 4
[96] Paul F. Brandwein; "The social sciences: concepts and values, Volume 6" Harcourt, Brace & World 1970 Page 389
[97] Skidmore, p. 154
[98] Skidmore, pp. 155–156
[99] Bueno, pp. 328 and 331
[100] Bradford Burns 1993, Ibidem p352
[101] Fausto (2005), p. 249
[102] Fausto (2005), p. 267
[103] Skidmore, p. 162
[104] Bueno, p. 336
[105] Skidmore, p. 164
[106] Patricia Baum; "Dictators of Latin America" Putnam 1972 Page 74
[107] Frank M. Colby, Allen L. Churchill, Herbert T. Wade & Frank H. Vizetelly; "The New international year book" Dodd, Mead & Co. 1989 Page 102 "The Fascist Revolt"
[108] David R. Mares; "Violent peace: militarized interstate bargaining in Latin America" Columbia University Press 2001 Chapter 5 Page 125
[109] Charles Howard Ellis; "The origin, structure & working of the League of Nations" The LawBook Exchange Ltd 2003 Pages: 105 3rd paragraph and 145 1st one
[110] Scheina, Robert L. Latin America's Wars Vol.II: The Age of the Professional Soldier, 1900–2001. Potomac Books, 2003 ISBN 1574884522 Part 4; Chapter 5 – World War I and Brazil, 1917–18
[111] M.Sharp, I.Westwell & J.Westwood; "History of World War I, Volume 1" Marshall Cavendish Corporation 2002 page 97
[112] Barman 1999, Ibidem Page405 2nd paragraph
[113] Mónica Hirst & Andrew Hurrell; "The United States and Brazil: a long road of unmet expectations" Taylor & Francis Books 2005 ISBN 0-415-95066-X Pages 4 & 5
[114] See Scheina, 2003 Part 9; Chapter 17 – World War II, Brazil and Mexico, 1942–45
[115] Thomas M. Leonard & John F. Bratzel; "Latin America during World War II" Rowman & Littlefield Publishers Inc. 2007 Page 150
[116] Fausto (2005), p. 281
[117] Skidmore, pp. 182–183
[118] Bueno, pp. 346–347
[119] Skidmore, pp. 188–194
[120] Skidmore, p. 201
[121] Skidmore, pp. 202–203
[122] Skidmore, p. 204
[123] Skidmore, pp. 204–205
[124] Skidmore, pp. 209–210
[125] Skidmore, p. 210
[126] Fausto (2005), p. 397
[127] Gaspari, *A Ditadura Envergonhada*, pp. 141–142.
[128] Gaspari, *A Ditadura Envergonhada*, p. 35.
[129] Elio Gaspari, *A ditadura escancarada* (São Paulo: Companhia das Letras, 2002), p. 193.
[130] Skidmore, p. 239
[131] Fausto (2005), p. 422
[132] Bueno, p. 379.

[133] Fausto (2005), p. 455.
[134] Gaspari, *A Ditadura Envergonhada*, pp. 34–35.
[135] Gaspari, *A Ditadura Envergonhada*, pp. 35–36.
[136] Bueno, p. 382.
[137] Fausto (2005), p. 460.
[138] Fausto (2005), pp. 464–465.
[139] Fausto (2005), pp. 465, 475.
[140] The name of the current Brazilian currency came both from the Real Unity of Value (a transition currency) and from an older currency that existed until 1942. In Portuguese it is called "Real", meaning "royal", as it originated in Portugal, then a monarchy (Skidmore, p. 311).
[141] Fausto (2005), p. 482.
[142] Fausto (2005), p. 474.
[143] Fausto (2005), p. 502.
[144] "Brazil elects Dilma Rousseff, nation's first woman president" (http://articles.cnn.com/2010-10-31/world/brazil.elections_1_voting-machines-president-luiz-inacio-manaus?_s=PM:WORLD). CNN. 2010-10-31. . Retrieved 2011-08-08.
[145] "Land and Resources" (http://www.webcitation.org/5kwQHrh6l). *Encarta*. MSN. Archived from the original (http://encarta.msn.com/encyclopedia_761554342/Brazil.html#s1) on 2009-10-31. . Retrieved 2008-06-11.
[146] Official Area (In Portuguese) (http://www.ibge.gov.br/home/geociencias/cartografia/default_territ_area.shtm) IBGE: Instituto Brasileiro de Geografia e Estatística. Retrieved 2010-01-08.
[147] "Natural Regions" (http://www.webcitation.org/5kwQHrh6l). *Encarta*. MSN. Archived from the original (http://encarta.msn.com/encyclopedia_761554342/Brazil.html#s1) on 2009-10-31. . Retrieved 2008-06-11.
[148] "Rivers and Lakes" (http://www.webcitation.org/5kwQHBKyV). *Encarta*. MSN. Archived from the original (http://encarta.msn.com/encyclopedia_761554342/Brazil.html) on 2009-10-31. . Retrieved 2008-06-11.
[149] "Brazil" (http://www.bbc.co.uk/weather/world/country_guides/results.shtml?tt=TT005220). *Country Guide*. BBC Weather. . Retrieved 2008-06-11.
[150] "Natural Regions" (http://www.webcitation.org/5kwQIOd3Z). *Encarta*. MSN. Archived from the original (http://encarta.msn.com/encyclopedia_761554342_2/Brazil.html) on 2009-10-31. . Retrieved 2008-06-11.
[151] "Temperature in Brazil" (http://www.v-brazil.com/information/geography/temperature-graphs.html). Brazil Travel. . Retrieved 2008-06-11.
[152] Embrapa. "Annual averages of Mandacaru Agro-meteorological station" (http://web.archive.org/web/20070820215606/http://www.cpatsa.embrapa.br/servicos/dadosmet/cem-anual.html) (in Portuguese). Archived from the original (http://www.cpatsa.embrapa.br/servicos/dadosmet/cem-anual.html) on 2007-08-20. . Retrieved 2008-10-21.
[153] "CPD: South America, Site SA19, Caatinga of North-eastern Brazil, Brazil" (http://botany.si.edu/projects/cpd/sa/sa19.htm). Botany.si.edu. . Retrieved 2009-10-29.
[154] " Drought, Smallpox, and Emergence of Leishmania braziliensis in Northeastern Brazil (http://origin.cdc.gov/eid/content/15/6/916.htm)." Centers for Disease Control and Prevention (CDC).
[155] " Ó Gráda, C.: Famine: A Short History (http://press.princeton.edu/chapters/s8857.html) " Princeton University Press.
[156] " Inland fishery enhancements (http://www.fao.org/DOCREP/005/W8514E/W8514E29.htm)." FAO.
[157] "One fifth of the world's freshwater" (http://www.panda.org/about_our_earth/about_freshwater/rivers/amazon/). *Amazon*. World Wide Fund for Nature. 2007-08-06. . Retrieved 2008-06-12.
[158] "Plant and Animal Life" (http://www.webcitation.org/5kwQIOd3Z). *Encarta*. MSN. Archived from the original (http://encarta.msn.com/encyclopedia_761554342_2/Brazil.html) on 2009-10-31. . Retrieved 2008-06-12.
[159] "Atlantic Forest, Brazil" (http://news.bbc.co.uk/2/hi/science/nature/3707888.stm#brazil). *Map: Biodiversity hotspots* (BBC News). 2004-10-01. . Retrieved 2008-06-12.
[160] "Environmental Issues" (http://www.webcitation.org/5kwQIOd3Z). *Encarta*. MSN. Archived from the original (http://encarta.msn.com/encyclopedia_761554342_2/Brazil.html) on 2009-10-31. . Retrieved 2008-06-12.
[161] "Under threat" (http://www.greenpeace.org/international/campaigns/forests/south-america/under-threat). Greenpeace. . Retrieved 2008-06-12.
[162] "Amazon destruction: six football fields a minute" (http://web.archive.org/web/20080405192352/http://www.greenpeace.org/international/news/amazon-destruction). Greenpeace. Archived from the original (http://www.greenpeace.org/international/news/amazon-destruction) on 2008-04-05. . Retrieved 2008-06-12.
[163] " Brazil grants environmental licence for Belo Monte dam (http://news.bbc.co.uk/2/hi/americas/8492577.stm)." *BBC News*. February 2, 2010.
[164] "Embassy of Brazil — Ottawa" (http://www.brasembottawa.org/en/brazil_in_brief/political_institution.html). . Retrieved 2007-07-19. "Political Institutions — The Executive"
[165] "City Mayors" (http://www.citymayors.com/government/brazil_government.html). . Retrieved 2007-07-19. "Brazil federal, state and local government"
[166] "JSTOR". JSTOR 196424). "Brazilian Politics"
[167] "Leftist Lula wins Brazil election" (http://news.bbc.co.uk/2/hi/americas/2367025.stm) BBC News. Accessed 17 May 2007

Brazil

[168] "Government – Brazil" (http://www.southtravels.com/america/brazil/government.html). Southtravels.com. 1988-10-05. . Retrieved 2010-03-17.
[169] "The Brazilian Legal System" (http://www.oas.org/juridico/mla/en/bra/en_bra-int-des-ordrjur.html), Organization of American States. Accessed 17 May 2007.
[170] José Afonso da Silva, *Curso de Direito Constitucional Positivo* (Malheiros, 2004; ISBN 85-7420-559-1), p. 46.
[171] Silva, *Curso de Direito Constitucional Positivo*, p. 592.
[172] "Government structure" (http://www.brasil.gov.br/ingles/about_brazil/government_structure/loren/) Brazilian Government. Accessed 17 May 2007.
[173] Miguel Glugoski and Odete Medauar, " Nossos direitos nas suas mãos (http://www.usp.br/jorusp/arquivo/2003/jusp667/pag0304.htm)," USP Journal, 24–30 November 2003. Retrieved 17 May 2007.
[174] Diego Abreu, " Primeira Corte do mundo a ter canal de vídeo no YouTube é o STF (http://g1.globo.com/Noticias/Brasil/0,,MUL1326475-5598,00.html)," G1 (http://g1.globo.com/). (**Portuguese**) Accessed October 12, 2009.
[175] " STF: Primeira corte do mundo no Youtube (http://esma.tjpb.jus.br/index.php?option=com_content&view=article&id=109:stf-primeira-corte-no-mundo-no-youtube&catid=1:noticias&Itemid=20)." ESMA-PB (http://esma.tjpb.jus.br/). (**Portuguese**) Accessed October 12, 2009.
[176] " Página do STF no Twitter está no ar (http://www.stf.jus.br/portal/cms/verNoticiaDetalhe.asp?idConteudo=117153)" (12/01/009). STF Official Website (http://www.stf.jus.br/). (**Portuguese**) Consulted on December 5, 2009.
[177] Kingstone, Steve (2005-06-27). "UN highlights Brazil gun crisis" (http://news.bbc.co.uk/2/hi/americas/4628813.stm). *BBC News*. . Retrieved 2010-04-30.
[178] Diego Abreu Do G1, em Brasília. "Number of people incarcerated in Brazil – 2010" (http://g1.globo.com/Noticias/Brasil/0,,MUL1500012-5598,00-GOVERNO+LANCA+ESTRATEGIA+PARA+DESARTICULAR+ORGANIZACOES+CRIMINOSAS.html). G1.globo.com. . Retrieved 2011-04-16.
[179] Maria Regina Soares de Lima and Mônica Hirst, " Brazil as a regional power: Action, choice and responsibilities (http://www3.interscience.wiley.com/journal/118726907/abstract?CRETRY=1&SRETRY=0)," *International Affairs* 82 (2006) 21–40. Retrieved June 22, 2007.
[180] Luiz Alberto Moniz Bandeira, " Brazil as a regional power (http://lap.sagepub.com/cgi/content/abstract/33/3/12)," Sage Journals Online. Retrieved June 22, 2007.
[181] Raúl Zibechi, " Difficult Path (http://www.fntg.org/fntg/docs/BrazilMultilateralism.pdf)" Funder's Network on Trade and Globalization. Retrieved June 22, 2007.
[182] Universia Knowledge at Wharton website, " Can Brazil Play a Leadership Role in the Current Round of Global Trade Talks? (http://www.wharton.universia.net/index.cfm?fa=viewfeature&id=1087&language=english)" Wharton School, Pennsylvania. Retrieved June 22, 2007.
[183] Clare Ribando, " US-Brazil relations (http://www.wilsoncenter.org/news/docs/RL33456.pdf)," Congressional Research Service. Retrieved on August 16, 2007.
[184] Georges D. Landau, "The Decisionmaking Process in Foreign Policy: The Case of Brazil," Center for Strategic and International Studies: Washington DC: March 2003.
[185] Raúl Zibechi, " Brazil and the Difficult Path to Multilateralism (http://www.fntg.org/fntg/docs/BrazilMultilateralism.pdf)." IRC Americas. Retrieved on August 16, 2007.
[186] Maria Regina Soares De Lima and Monica Hirst, " Brazil as an intermediate state and regional power: action, choice and responsibilities (http://www.blackwell-synergy.com/doi/abs/10.1111/j.1468-2346.2006.00513.x)," *International Affairs* 82 (1), 21–40. Retrieved on August 16, 2007.
[187] Luiz Alberto Moniz Bandeira, " Brazil as a Regional Power and Its Relations with the United States (http://lap.sagepub.com/cgi/content/abstract/33/3/12)," University of Brasília. Retrieved on August 16, 2007.
[188] Cabral and Weinstock 2010. Brazil: an emerging aid player (http://www.odi.org.uk/resources/details.asp?id=5120&title=brazil-election-emerging-donor-aid). London: Overseas Development Institute
[189] Cabral, Lidia 2010. Brazil's development cooperation with the South: a global model in waiting (http://blogs.odi.org.uk/blogs/main/archive/2010/07/22/brazil_south_south_cooperation.aspx). London: Overseas Development Institute
[190] "Pesquisa mostra que Brasil investe pouco em estratégia na FAB" (http://g1.globo.com/jornaldaglobo/0,,MUL1412734-16021,00-PESQUISA+MOSTRA+QUE+BRASIL+INVESTE+POUCO+EM+ESTRATEGIA+NA+FAB.html) (in Portuguese). G1.com.br. . Retrieved 2010-10-02.
[191] "Brazil: Military: Introduction" (http://www.globalsecurity.org/military/world/brazil/intro.htm). GlobalSecurity.org. . Retrieved 2010-10-02.
[192] "Decreto Nº 5.670 de 10 de Janeiro de 2006" (http://www.planalto.gov.br/ccivil_03/_Ato2004-2006/2006/Decreto/D5670.htm) (in Portuguese). Presidência da República. . Retrieved 2010-10-02.
[193] "Perguntas" (https://www.mar.mil.br/menu_v/ccsm/perguntas/perguntas_mais_frequentes.htm#44.44) (in Portuguese). Marinha do Brasil. . Retrieved 2007-08-16.
[194] "Sala de imprensa – FAB em números" (http://www.fab.mil.br/portal/imprensa/fab_numeros.php) (in Portuguese). Força Aérea Brasileira. . Retrieved 2007-12-12.
[195] *The N-11: More Than an Acronym* (http://www.chicagobooth.edu/alumni/clubs/pakistan/docs/next11dream-march '07-goldmansachs.pdf). Goldman Sachs. . Retrieved 2010-03-17.

[196] "Economy of Brazil" (https://www.cia.gov/library/publications/the-world-factbook/geos/br.html). Central Intelligence Agency. 2008. . Retrieved 2008-06-03.
[197] Phillips, Tom (2008-05-10). "The country of the future finally arrives" (http://www.guardian.co.uk/world/2008/may/10/brazil.oil). *The Guardian* (London). . Retrieved 2008-06-06.
[198] "The economy of heat" (http://www.economist.com/surveys/displaystory.cfm?story_id=8952496). The Economist. 2007-04-12. . Retrieved 2008-06-06.
[199] O'Neill, Jim. "BRICs" (http://www2.goldmansachs.com/ideas/brics/index.html). Goldman Sachs. . Retrieved 2008-06-06.
[200] Baig, Taimur; Goldfajn, Ilan (2000). "The Russian default and the contagion to Brazil" (http://www.imf.org/external/pubs/ft/wp/2000/wp00160.pdf) (PDF). *IMF Working Paper*. International Monetary Fund. . Retrieved 2008-06-06.
[201] Fraga, Arminio (2000). "Monetary Policy During the Transition to a Floating Exchange Rate: Brazil's Recent Experience" (http://www.imf.org/external/pubs/ft/fandd/2000/03/fraga.htm). International Monetary Fund. . Retrieved 2008-06-06.
[202] "Brasil supera Canadá e se torna o terceiro maior exportador agrícola" (http://www.estadao.com.br/estadaodehoje/20100307/not_imp520620,0.php). O Estado de S. Paulo. 2010-03-07. . Retrieved 2010-03-07.
[203] Wheatley, Jonathan (2002-09-02). "Brazil: When an IMF Bailout Is Not Enough" (http://www.businessweek.com/magazine/content/02_35/b3797071.htm). Business Week. . Retrieved 2008-06-06.
[204] "Brazil to pay off IMF debts early" (http://news.bbc.co.uk/2/hi/business/4527438.stm). BBC News. 2005-12-14. . Retrieved 2008-06-06.
[205] "Economic Quarterly" (http://www.ipea.gov.br/sites/000/2/publicacoes/eqb/ieq11.pdf) (PDF). Institute of Applied Economic Research. 2007-03-01. pp. 171. . Retrieved 2008-06-06.
[206] "Capital Flows to Emerging Markets Set at Close to Record Levels" (http://www.iif.com/press/press+32.php) (Press release). The Institute of International Finance. 2007-05-31. . Retrieved 2008-06-06.
[207] "IPCA, IPC-FIPE and IPC-BR: Methodological and Empirical Differences" (http://www.bcb.gov.br/htms/relinf/ing/2004/06/ri200406b2i.pdf) (PDF). Central Bank of Brazil. 2004. . Retrieved 2008-06-06.
[208] "Statistics on Mergers & Acquisitions (M&A) – M&A Courses | Company Valuation Courses | Mergers & Acquisitions Courses" (http://www.imaa-institute.org/statistics-mergers-acquisitions.html#MergersAcquisitions_Brazil). Imaa-institute.org. . Retrieved 2011-04-16.
[209] Rousseff Crisis Spurred by Lula Debts as Brazil Boom Diminishes- Bloomberg (http://mobile.bloomberg.com/news/2011-09-27/rousseff-crisis-spurred-by-lula-debts-as-brazil-boom-diminishes)
[210] "Brazil's shares at all-time high" (http://news.bbc.co.uk/2/hi/business/7376539.stm). BBC News. 2008-04-30. . Retrieved 2008-06-09.
[211] Alves, Fabio; Caminada, Carlos (2008-04-30). "Brazilian Debt Raised to Investment Grade by S&P" (http://www.bloomberg.com/apps/news?pid=20601086&sid=a86v4f6_W2Jg). Reuters. . Retrieved 2008-06-09.
[212] Warner, Jeremy (2008-05-02). "Jeremy Warner's Outlook: Brazil secures investment grade" (http://www.independent.co.uk/news/business/comment/jeremy-warner/jeremy-warners-outlook-brazil-secures-investment-grade-819744.html). London: The Independent. . Retrieved 2008-06-09.
[213] Colitt, Raymond (2008-05-13). "Sleeping giant Brazil wakes, but could stumble" (http://www.reuters.com/article/managerViews/idUSNOA33289320080513). Reuters. . Retrieved 2008-06-09.
[214] "Field Listing – GDP – composition by sector" (https://www.cia.gov/library/publications/the-world-factbook/fields/2012.html). Central Intelligence Agency. 2008. . Retrieved 2008-06-09.
[215] "Agriculture and Cattle-raising" (http://www.brasil.gov.br/ingles/about_brazil/brasil_topics/). *Brazil by Topics*. Brazilian Government official website. . Retrieved 2008-06-09.
[216] "Agriculture" (http://www.webcitation.org/5kwQKc5zk). *Encarta*. MSN. Archived from the original (http://encarta.msn.com/encyclopedia_761554342_6/Brazil.html) on 2009-10-31. . Retrieved 2008-06-09.
[217] "Manufacturing" (http://www.webcitation.org/5kwQKc5zk). *Encarta*. MSN. Archived from the original (http://encarta.msn.com/encyclopedia_761554342_6/Brazil.html) on 2009-10-31. . Retrieved 2008-06-09.
[218] "Energy" (http://www.webcitation.org/5kwQLDx9v). *Encarta*. MSN. Archived from the original (http://encarta.msn.com/encyclopedia_761554342_7/Brazil.html) on 2009-10-31. . Retrieved 2008-06-09.
[219] Moffett, Matt (2008-05-13). "Brazil Joins Front Rank Of New Economic Powers" (http://online.wsj.com/article/SB121063846832986909.html). The Wall Street Journal. . Retrieved 2008-06-09.
[220] "An economic superpower, and now oil too" (http://www.economist.com/opinion/displaystory.cfm?story_id=11052873). The Economist. 2008-04-17. . Retrieved 2008-06-09.
[221] Schneyer, Joshua (2007-11-09). "Brazil, the New Oil Superpower" (http://www.businessweek.com/bwdaily/dnflash/content/nov2007/db20071115_045316.htm?chan=top+news_top+news+index_businessweek+exclusives). Business Week. . Retrieved 2008-06-09.
[222] "More bounty" (http://www.economist.com/displaystory.cfm?story_id=11049391). The Economist. 2008-04-17. . Retrieved 2008-06-09.
[223] "Focus on Brazil" (http://www.worldenergyoutlook.org/docs/weo2006/brazil.pdf) (PDF). *World Energy Outlook*. International Energy Agency. 2006. . Retrieved 2008-12-14.
[224] "Project Closing Report. Natural Gas Centre of Excellence Project. Narrative" (http://web.archive.org/web/20070927192628/http://www.ctgas.com.br/conteudo/img_upload/Project_cloning_report_Narrative_Mar_20_05.pdf) (PDF). March 20, 2005. Archived from the original (http://www.ctgas.com.br/conteudo/img_upload/Project_cloning_report_Narrative_Mar_20_05.pdf) on 2007-09-27. . Retrieved

2007-05-12.

[225] Brazilian Government. "Skills training for growth" (http://www.brasil.gov.br/ingles/about_brazil/brasil_topics/science/categoria_view). . Retrieved 2007-08-10.

[226] "Brazil — The Space Program" (http://www.country-data.com/cgi-bin/query/r-1826.html). *country-data.com*. April 1997. . Retrieved 2008-05-24.

[227] "Confirmed: Agreement with France Includes the Brazilian Nuclear Submarine" (http://npsglobal.org/eng/index.php/highlight/13-news/351-confirmed-agreement-with-france-includes-the-brazilian-nuclear-submarine). *Nonproliferation for Global Security Foundation*. 2008-12-23. . Retrieved 2008-12-23.

[228] "Rheinische Friedrich-Wilhelms-Universität" (http://www-elsa.physik.uni-bonn.de/accelerator_list.html). Elsa.physik.uni-bonn.de. 2008-08-18. . Retrieved 2010-10-30.

[229] "CEITEC – Portal Brasil" (http://www.brasil.gov.br/sobre/science-and-technology/the-digital-electronics-industry/ceitec/br_model1?set_language=en). Brasil.gov.br. . Retrieved 2011-08-08.

[230] "Road system in Brazil" (http://www.nationsencyclopedia.com/Americas/Brazil-TRANSPORTATION.html). Nationsencyclopedia.com. . Retrieved 2010-10-30.

[231] " Brazil – Transportation (http://www.nationsencyclopedia.com/Americas/Brazil-TRANSPORTATION.html)," Encyclopedia of the Nations (nationsencyclopedia.com).

[232] " Ociosidade atinge 70% dos principais aeroportos (http://g1.globo.com/Noticias/Brasil/0,,MUL86760-5598,00.html)." globo.com, 12 August 2007. **(Portuguese)**

[233] " Aeroporto Internacional de São Paulo/Guarulhos-Governador André Franco Montoro (http://www.infraero.gov.br/aero_prev_home.php?ai=43)," infraaero.gov.br. **(Portuguese)**

[234] " Mercado Brasileiro Terminais de Contêineres (http://www.mzweb.com.br/santosbrasil/web/conteudo_pt.asp?idioma=0&tipo=3958&conta=28)," Santos Brasil. **(Portuguese)**

[235] Tendências Demográficas: Uma análise da população com base nos resultados dos Censos Demográficos 1940 e 2000 (http://www.ibge.gov.br/home/estatistica/populacao/tendencia_demografica/analise_populacao/1940_2000/default.shtm)

[236] Censo demográfico revela que o Brasil ficou mais velho e menos branco (http://port.pravda.ru/sociedade/curiosas/04-05-2011/31548-censo_demografico-0/)

[237] População que se declara branca diminui, diz IBGE (http://www.fatimanews.com.br/noticias/populacao-que-se-declara-branca-diminui-diz-ibge_116224/)

[238] 2008 PNAD, IBGE. " População residente por situação, sexo e grupos de idade (http://www.sidra.ibge.gov.br/bda/tabela/protabl.asp?c=261&i=P&nome=on&notarodape=on&tab=261&unit=0&pov=1&opc1=1&poc2=1&OpcTipoNivt=1&opn1=2&nivt=0&poc1=1&sec58=0&orp=6&qtu3=27&opv=1&sec1=0&opc2=1&pop1&opn2=2&orv=2&orc2=4&opc58=1&qtu2=5&sev=93&sec2=0&opp=1&opn3=0&orc1=3&poc58=1&qtu1=1&cabec=on&orc58=5&opn7=0&decm=0&ascendente=on&sep=43343&orn=1&qtu7=9&pon=2&OpcCara=44&proc=1)"

[239] 2008 PNAD, IBGE. " População residente por situação, sexo e grupos de idade (http://www.sidra.ibge.gov.br/bda/tabela/protabl.asp?c=261&i=P&nome=on&notarodape=on&tab=261&unit=0&pov=1&opc1=1&poc2=3&OpcTipoNivt=1&opn1=2&nivt=0&poc1=1&sec58=0&orp=6&qtu3=27&opv=1&sec1=0&opc2=1&pop1&opn2=2&orv=2&orc2=3&opc58=1&qtu2=5&sev=93&sec2=0&sec2=92956&sec2=92957&opp=1&opn3=0&orc1=3&poc58=1&qtu1=1&cabec=on&orc58=5&opn7=0&decm=99&ascendente=on&sep=43343&orn=1&qtu7=9&pon=2&OpcCara=44&proc=1)"

[240] 2008 PNAD, IBGE. " População residente por situação, sexo e grupos de idade (http://www.sidra.ibge.gov.br/bda/tabela/protabl.asp?c=261&i=P&nome=on&notarodape=on&tab=261&unit=0&pov=1&opc1=1&poc2=1&OpcTipoNivt=1&opn1=1&nivt=0&poc1=2&sec58=0&orp=6&qtu3=27&opv=1&sec1=0&sec1=1&sec1=2&opc2=1&pop=1&opn2=2&orv=2&orc2=4&opc58=1&qtu2=5&sev=93&sev=1000093&sec2=0&opp=1&opn3=0&orc1=3&poc58=1&qtu1=1&cabec=on&orc58=5&opn7=0&decm=99&ascendente=on&sep=43343&orn=1&qtu7=9&pon=2&OpcCara=44&proc=1)."

[241] " Brazil population reaches 190.8 million (http://www.brasil.gov.br/news/history/2011/04-1/29/brazil-population-reaches-190.8-million/newsitem_view?set_language=en)". Brasil.gov.br.

[242] " Shaping Brazil: The Role of International Migration (http://www.migrationinformation.org/profiles/display.cfm?id=311)". Migration Policy Institute.

[243] José Alberto Magno de Carvalho, " Crescimento populacional e estrutura demográfica no Brasil (http://www.observasaude.sp.gov.br/BibliotecaPortal/Acervo/Estrutura_DemogrÃ¡fica_Brasil.pdf)" Belo Horizonte: UFMG/Cedeplar, 2004 (PDF file), p. 5.

[244] "Instituto Brasileiro de Geografia e Estatística" (http://www.ibge.gov.br/home/presidencia/noticias/noticia_visualiza.php?id_noticia=1275&id_pagina=1). IBGE. 1999-11-29. . Retrieved 2010-01-25.

[245] "Projeyco da Populayco do Brasil" (http://www.ibge.gov.br/home/presidencia/noticias/noticia_impressao.php?id_noticia=1272). IBGE. . Retrieved 2010-01-25.

[246] Magno de Carvalho, " Crescimento populacional e estrutura demográfica no Brasil (http://www.observasaude.sp.gov.br/BibliotecaPortal/Acervo/Estrutura_DemogrÃ¡fica_Brasil.pdf)," pp. 7–8.

[247] 2008 PNAD, IBGE. " População residente por cor ou raça, situação e sexo (http://www.sidra.ibge.gov.br/bda/tabela/protabl.asp?c=262&i=P&nome=on&notarodape=on&tab=262&unit=0&pov=3&opc1=1&poc2=1&OpcTipoNivt=1&opn1=2&nivt=0&orc86=3&poc1=1&orp=6&qtu3=27&opv=1&poc86=2&sec1=0&opc2=1&pop=1&opn2=0&orv=2&orc2=5&qtu2=5&sev=93&sev=1000093&opc86=1&sec2=0&opp=1&opn3=0&sec86=0&sec86=2776&sec86=2777&sec86=2779&sec86=2778&sec86=2780&

sec86=2781&ascendente=on&sep=43344&orn=1&qtu7=9&orc1=4&qtu1=1&cabec=on&pon=1&OpcCara=44&proc=1&opn7=0&decm=99)."
[248] " In Amazonia, Defending the Hidden Tribes (http://www.washingtonpost.com/wp-dyn/content/article/2007/07/07/AR2007070701312.html)," *The Washington Post*, 8 July 2007.
[249] *Enciclopédia Barsa* vol. 4, p. 230.
[250] Coelho (1996), p. 268.
[251] Vesentini (1988), p. 117.
[252] Adas, Melhem. *Panorama geográfico do Brasil*, 4th ed (São Paulo: Moderna, 2004), p. 268
[253] Azevedo (1971), pp. 2–3.
[254] Moreira (1981), p. 108.
[255] *Enciclopédia Barsa*, vol. 4, pp. 254–55, 258, 265.
[256] Azevedo (1971), pp. 74–75.
[257] *Enciclopédia Barsa*, vol. 10 (Rio de Janeiro: Encyclopaedia Britannica do Brasil, 1987), p. 355.
[258] Azevedo (1971), p. 74.
[259] Azevedo (1971), p. 161.
[260] Maria Stella Ferreira-Levy, "O papel da migração internacional na evolução da população brasileira (1872 a 1972), *Revista de Saúde Pública* Volume 8, suplemento. June 1974.) (1974). Table 2, p. 74. (**Portuguese**) available on scielo.br (http://www.scielo.br/pdf/rsp/v8s0/03.pdf) as a PDF file.
[261] PNAD 2008, IBGE. " Pessoas de 5 anos ou mais de idade por situação, sexo, alfabetização e grupos de idade e grupos de idade (http://www.sidra.ibge.gov.br/bda/tabela/protabl.asp?c=271&i=P&sec59=93024&sec59=1023&sec59=1024&nome=on&notarodape=on&tab=271&unit=0&pov=3&opc1=1&poc2=1&orc59=5&OpcTipoNivt=1&opn1=2&nivt=0&poc1=1&sec58=0&orp=7&qtu3=27&opv=1&sec1=0&opc2=1&pop=1&opn2=2&orv=2&orc2=4&opc58=1&qtu2=5&sev=121&sev=1000121&sec2=0&poc59=2&opp=1&opn3=0&orc1=3&poc58=1&qtu1=1&cabec=on&opc59=1&ascendente=on&sep=43345&orn=1&qtu7=9&orc58=6&opn7=0&decm=99&pon=1&OpcCara=44&proc=1)."
[262] PNAD 2008, IBGE. " Pessoas de 5 anos ou mais de idade por situação, sexo, alfabetização e grupos de idade (http://www.sidra.ibge.gov.br/bda/tabela/protabl.asp?c=271&i=P&sec59=93024&sec59=1023&sec59=1024&nome=on&notarodape=on&tab=271&unit=0&pov=3&opc1=1&poc2=1&orc59=5&OpcTipoNivt=1&opn1=2&nivt=0&poc1=1&sec58=0&orp=7&qtu3=27&opv=1&sec1=0&opc2=1&pop=1&opn2=2&orv=2&orc2=4&opc58=1&qtu2=5&sev=121&sev=1000121&sec2=0&poc59=3&opp=1&opn3=0&orc1=3&poc58=1&qtu1=1&cabec=on&opc59=1&ascendente=on&sep=43345&orn=1&qtu7=9&orc58=6&opn7=0&decm=99&pon=2&OpcCara=44&proc=1)"
[263] PNAD 2008, IBGE. " Pessoas de 5 anos ou mais de idade por situação, sexo e alfabetização (http://www.sidra.ibge.gov.br/bda/tabela/protabl.asp?c=2858&i=P&sec59=0&sec59=1023&sec59=1024&sec59=3318&nome=on&notarodape=on&tab=2858&unit=0&pov=1&opc1=1&poc2=1&orc59=5&OpcTipoNivt=1&opn1=2&nivt=0&poc1=2&orp=6&qtu3=27&opv=1&sec1=0&sec1=1&sec1=2&opc2=1&pop=1&opn2=0&orv=2&orc2=4&opc58=1&sev=121&sec2=0&poc59=3&opp=1&opn3=0&orc1=3&qtu1=1&cabec=on&opc59=1&ascendente=on&sep=43345&orn=1&qtu7=9&pon=1&OpcCara=44&proc=1&opn7=0&decm=99)."
[264] IBGE, *População residente, por sexo e situação do domicílio, segundo a religião* (http://www.ibge.gov.br/home/estatistica/populacao/censo2000/populacao/religiao_Censo2000.pdf), Censo Demográfico 2000. Acessado em 13 de dezembro de 2007
[265] "Brazil" (http://berkleycenter.georgetown.edu/resources/countries/brazil). Berkley Center for Religion, Peace, and World Affairs. . Retrieved 2011-12-07.
[266] "Brazil" (http://www.state.gov/g/drl/rls/irf/2005/51629.htm). *International Religious Freedom Report*. U.S. Department of State. 2005-11-08. . Retrieved 2008-06-08.
[267] "Brazil" (http://berkleycenter.georgetown.edu/resources/countries/brazil). Berkley Center for Religion, Peace, and World Affairs. . Retrieved 2011-12-07. See drop-down essay on "The Growth of Religious Pluralism"
[268] (http://g1.globo.com/brasil/noticia/2011/08/pais-tem-menor-nivel-de-adeptos-do-catolicismo-desde-1872-diz-estudo.html)
[269] "IDBGE" (http://www.ibge.gov.br/home/estatistica/populacao/censo2010/default.shtm). IBGE. 2011. . Retrieved 2011-10-08. (**Portuguese**)
[270] 2008 PNAD, IBGE. " População residente por situação, sexo e grupos de idade (http://www.sidra.ibge.gov.br/bda/tabela/protabl.asp?c=261&i=P&nome=on&notarodape=on&tab=261&unit=0&pov=1&opc1=1&poc2=1&opn1=2&OpcTipoNivt=2&nivt=0&poc1=1&sec58=0&orp=6&qtu3=27&opv=1&sec1=0&opc2=1&pop=1&opn2=0&orv=2&orc2=4&opc58=1&qtu2=5&sev=93&sec2=0&opp=1&opn3=0&orc1=3&poc58=1&qtu1=1&cabec=on&orc58=5&opn7=0&decm=99&ascendente=on&sep=43343&orn=1&qtu7=9&pon=2&OpcCara=43&proc=1)."
[271] "Principal Cities" (http://www.webcitation.org/5kwQIvYDr). *Encarta*. MSN. Archived from the original (http://encarta.msn.com/encyclopedia_761554342_3/Brazil.html) on 2009-10-31. . Retrieved 2008-06-10.
[272] Rohter, Larry (2005-08-28). "Language Born of Colonialism Thrives Again in Amazon" (http://www.nytimes.com/2005/08/28/international/americas/28amazon.html?ex=1282881600&en=2dbb31357d010164&ei=5090). New York Times. . Retrieved 2008-07-14.
[273] "Portuguese language and the Brazilian singularity" (http://countrystudies.us/brazil/39.htm). .
[274] (http://www.sibila.com.br/index.php/world-map-of-portuguese/424)
[275] "Languages of Brazil" (http://www.ethnologue.com/show_country.asp?name=br). Ethnologue. . Retrieved 2008-06-09.

[276] Nash, Elizabeth (2008-05-02). "Portugal pays lip service to Brazil's supremacy" (http://www.independent.co.uk/news/world/europe/portugal-pays-lip-service-to-brazils-supremacy-819728.html). London: The Independent. . Retrieved 2008-06-09.
[277] "O alemão lusitano do Sul do Brasil" (http://www.dw-world.de/dw/article/0,,1174391,00.html). DW-World.de. .
[278] "O talian" (http://www.labeurb.unicamp.br/elb/europeias/talian.htm). .
[279] "Esperanto approved by Brazilian government as optional high school subject, mandatory if justified by demand" (http://www.pagef30.com/2009/09/15-september-2009-esperanto-approved-by.html). Page F30. 2009-09-19. . Retrieved 2010-10-30.
[280] "15th–16th Century" (http://www.brasil.gov.br/ingles/about_brazil/history/xvi_cent/). *History*. Brazilian Government official website. . Retrieved 2008-06-08.
[281] "People and Society" (http://www.webcitation.org/5kwQIvYDr). *Encarta*. MSN. Archived from the original (http://encarta.msn.com/encyclopedia_761554342_3/Brazil.html) on 2009-10-31. . Retrieved 2008-06-10.
[282] "Population" (http://www.webcitation.org/5kwQIvYDr). *Encarta*. MSN. Archived from the original (http://encarta.msn.com/encyclopedia_761554342_3/Brazil.html) on 2009-10-31. . Retrieved 2008-06-10.
[283] Freyre, Gilberto (1986). "The Afro-Brazilian experiment: African influence on Brazilian culture" (http://findarticles.com/p/articles/mi_m1310/is_1986_May-June/ai_4375022). UNESCO. . Retrieved 2008-06-08.
[284] Candido; Antonio. (1970) *Vários escritos*. São Paulo: Duas Cidades. p.18
[285] Leandro Karnal, *Teatro da fé: Formas de representação religiosa no Brasil e no México do século XVI*, São Paulo, Editora Hucitec, 1998; available on fflch.usp.br (http://www.fflch.usp.br/dh/ceveh/public_html/biblioteca/livros/teatro_fe/index.htm)
[286] " The Brazilian Baroque (http://www.itaucultural.org.br/aplicExternas/enciclopedia_IC/index.cfm?fuseaction=termos_texto_ing&cd_verbete=3738&lst_palavras=&cd_idioma=28556&cd_item=8)," *Encyclopaedia Itaú Cultural*
[287] "Theater and Film" (http://www.webcitation.org/5kwQK47Yx). *Encarta*. MSN. Archived from the original (http://encarta.msn.com/encyclopedia_761554342_5/Brazil.html) on 2009-10-31. . Retrieved 2008-06-08.
[288] "Literature" (http://www.webcitation.org/5kwQK47Yx). *Encarta*. MSN. Archived from the original (http://encarta.msn.com/encyclopedia_761554342_5/Brazil.html) on 2009-10-31. . Retrieved 2008-06-08.
[289] " Brazilian Literature: An Introduction (http://www.brasembottawa.org/en/culture_academic/literature.html)." Embassy of Brasil – Ottawa (http://www.brasembottawa.org/). Visited on November 2, 2009.
[290] "Way of Life" (http://www.webcitation.org/5kwQJT42w). *Encarta*. MSN. Archived from the original (http://encarta.msn.com/encyclopedia_761554342_4/Brazil.html) on 2009-10-31. . Retrieved 2008-06-08.
[291] Roger, " Feijoada: The Brazilian national dish (http://www.braziltravelguide.com/feijoada-the-brazilian-national-dish.html)" braziltravelguide.com.
[292] Cascudo, Luis da Câmara. História da Alimentação no Brasil. São Paulo/Belo Horizonte: Editora USP/Itatiaia, l983.
[293] Freyre, Gilberto. Açúcar. Uma Sociologia do Doce, com Receitas de Bolos e Doces do Nordeste do Brasil. São Paulo, Companhia das Letras, 1997.
[294] Barbosa, Lívia. Feijão com arroz e arroz com feijão: o Brasil no prato dos brasileiros. Horiz. antropol. [online]. 2007, vol.13, n.28 [cited 2011-03-09], pp. 87–116 . Available from: scielo.br (http://www.scielo.br/scielo.php?script=sci_arttext&pid=S0104-71832007000200005&lng=en&nrm=iso) ISSN 0104-7183. doi: 10.1590/S0104-71832007000200005.
[295] Ferraccioli, Patrícia; Silveira, Eliane Augusta da.(2010) Cultural feeding influence on palative memories in the usual brazilian cuisine. Rev. enferm. UERJ;18(2):198–203, abr.-jun. 2010. (http://bases.bireme.br/cgi-bin/wxislind.exe/iah/online/?IsisScript=iah/iah.xis&src=google&base=BDENF&lang=p&nextAction=lnk&exprSearch=18716&indexSearch=ID)
[296] "Futebol, o esporte mais popular do Brasil, é destaque no Via Legal :: Notícias" (http://www.jusbrasil.com.br/noticias/74894/futebol-o-esporte-mais-popular-do-brasil-e-destaque-no-via-legal). Jusbrasil.com.br. . Retrieved 2011-04-16.
[297] "Football in Brazil" (http://www.fifa.com/associations/association=bra/goalprogramme/index.html). *Goal Programme*. International Federation of Association Football. 2008-04-15. . Retrieved 2008-06-06.
[298] "Beach Soccer" (http://www.fifa.com/aboutfifa/developing/beachsoccer/index.html). International Federation of Association Football. . Retrieved 2008-06-06.
[299] "Futsal" (http://www.fifa.com/aboutfifa/developing/futsal/index.html). International Federation of Association Football. . Retrieved 2008-06-06.
[300] "The art of capoeira" (http://www.bbc.co.uk/northyorkshire/content/articles/2005/09/13/capoeira_feature.shtml). BBC. 2006-09-20. . Retrieved 2008-06-06.
[301] "Brazilian Vale Tudo" (http://valetudo.com.br/). I.V.C. . Retrieved 2008-06-06.
[302] "Brazilian Jiu-Jitsu Official Website" (http://www.ibjjf.org/index.htm). International Brazilian Jiu-Jitsu Federation. . Retrieved 2008-06-06.
[303] Donaldson, Gerald. "Emerson Fittipaldi" (http://www.formula1.com/teams_and_drivers/hall_of_fame/282/). *Hall of Fame*. The Official Formula 1 Website. . Retrieved 2008-06-06.
[304] Donaldson, Gerald. "Nelson Piquet" (http://www.formula1.com/teams_and_drivers/hall_of_fame/181/). *Hall of Fame*. The Official Formula 1 Website. . Retrieved 2008-06-06.
[305] Donaldson, Gerald. "Ayrton Senna" (http://www.formula1.com/teams_and_drivers/hall_of_fame/45/). *Hall of Fame*. The Official Formula 1 Website. . Retrieved 2008-06-06.
[306] "1950 FIFA World Cup Brazil" (http://www.fifa.com/worldcup/archive/edition=7/index.html). *Previous FIFA World Cups*. International Federation of Association Football. . Retrieved 2008-06-06.

[307] "2014 FIFA World Cup Brazil" (http://www.fifa.com/worldcup/brazil2014/index.html). International Federation of Association Football. . Retrieved 2008-06-06.
[308] "Formula 1 Grande Premio do Brasil 2008" (http://www.formula1.com/races/in_detail/brazil_804/circuit_diagram.html). The Official Formula 1 Website. . Retrieved 2008-06-06.
[309] "Chronological list of Pan American Games" (http://odepapaso.org/paso/chrono.html). Pan American Sports Organization. . Retrieved 2008-06-06.
[310] " Olympics 2016: Tearful Pele and weeping Lula greet historic win for Rio (http://www.guardian.co.uk/sport/2009/oct/02/olympics-2016-games-rio-pele)," *The Guardian*, 2 October 2009.
[311] "Brazil launches international TV station for Africa" (http://news.bbc.co.uk/2/hi/world/latin_america/10152301.stm). BBC News. 2010-05-25. . Retrieved 2010-10-30.

Bibliographic

- Azevedo, Aroldo. *O Brasil e suas regiões*. São Paulo: Companhia Editora Nacional, 1971. (Portuguese)
- Barman, Roderick J. *Citizen Emperor: Pedro II and the Making of Brazil, 1825–1891*. Stanford: Stanford University Press, 1999. ISBN 0-8047-3510-7 (English)
- Boxer, Charles R.. *O império marítimo português 1415–1825*. São Paulo: Companhia das Letras, 2002. ISBN 8535902929 (Portuguese)
- Bueno, Eduardo. *Brasil: uma História*. São Paulo: Ática, 2003. (Portuguese) ISBN 8508082134
- Calmon, Pedro. *História da Civilização Brasileira*. Brasília: Senado Federal, 2002. (Portuguese)
- Carvalho, José Murilo de. *D. Pedro II*. São Paulo: Companhia das Letras, 2007. (Portuguese)
- Coelho, Marcos Amorim. *Geografia do Brasil*. 4th ed. São Paulo: Moderna, 1996. (Portuguese)
- Diégues, Fernando. *A revolução brasílica*. Rio de Janeiro: Objetiva, 2004. (Portuguese)
- *Enciclopédia Barsa*. Volume 4: Batráquio – Camarão, Filipe. Rio de Janeiro: Encyclopædia Britannica do Brasil, 1987. (Portuguese)
- Fausto, Boris and Devoto, Fernando J. *Brasil e Argentina: Um ensaio de história comparada (1850–2002)*, 2nd ed. São Paulo: Editoria 34, 2005. ISBN 8573263083(Portuguese)
- Gaspari, Elio. *A ditadura envergonhada*. São Paulo: Companhia das Letras, 2002. ISBN 8535902775 (Portuguese)
- Janotti, Aldo. *O Marquês de Paraná: inícios de uma carreira política num momento crítico da história da nacionalidade*. Belo Horizonte: Itatiaia, 1990. (Portuguese)
- Lyra, Heitor. *História de Dom Pedro II (1825–1891): Ascenção (1825–1870)*. v.1. Belo Horizonte: Itatiaia, 1977. (Portuguese)
- Lyra, Heitor. *História de Dom Pedro II (1825–1891): Declínio (1880–1891)*. v.3. Belo Horizonte: Itatiaia, 1977. (Portuguese)
- Lustosa, Isabel. *D. Pedro I: um herói sem nenhum caráter*. São Paulo: Companhia das letras, 2006. ISBN 8535908072 (Portuguese)
- Moreira, Igor A. G. *O Espaço Geográfico, geografia geral e do Brasil*. 18. Ed. São Paulo: Ática, 1981. (Portuguese)
- Munro, Dana Gardner. *The Latin American Republics; A History*. New York: D. Appleton, 1942. (English)
- Schwarcz, Lilia Moritz. *As barbas do Imperador: D. Pedro II, um monarca nos trópicos*. 2nd ed. São Paulo: Companhia das Letras, 1998. ISBN 8571648379 (Portuguese)
- Skidmore, Thomas E. *Uma História do Brasil*. 4th ed. São Paulo: Paz e Terra, 2003. (Portuguese) ISBN 8521903138
- Souza, Adriana Barreto de. *Duque de Caxias: o homem por trás do monumento*. Rio de Janeiro: Civilização Brasileira, 2008. (Portuguese) ISBN 9788520008645
- Vainfas, Ronaldo. *Dicionário do Brasil Imperial*. Rio de Janeiro: Objetiva, 2002. ISBN 8573024410 (Portuguese)
- Vesentini, José William. *Brasil, sociedade e espaço – Geografia do Brasil*. 7th Ed. São Paulo: Ática, 1988. (Portuguese)

- Vianna, Hélio. *História do Brasil: período colonial, monarquia e república*, 15th ed. São Paulo: Melhoramentos, 1994. (Portuguese)

Further reading

- Alves, Maria Helena Moreira (1985). *State and Opposition in Military Brazil*. Austin, TX: University of Texas Press.
- Amann, Edmund (1990). *The Illusion of Stability: The Brazilian Economy under Cardoso*. World Development (pp. 1805–1819).
- "Background Note: Brazil" (http://www.state.gov/r/pa/ei/bgn/35640.htm). US Department of State. Retrieved 2011-06-16.
- Bellos, Alex (2003). *Futebol: The Brazilian Way of Life*. London: Bloomsbury Publishing plc.
- Bethell, Leslie (1991). *Colonial Brazil*. Cambridge: CUP.
- Costa, João Cruz (1964). *A History of Ideas in Brazil*. Los Angeles, CA: University of California Press.
- Fausto, Boris (1999). *A Concise History of Brazil*. Cambridge: CUP.
- Furtado, Celso. *The Economic Growth of Brazil: A Survey from Colonial to Modern Times*. Berkeley, CA: University of California Press.
- Leal, Victor Nunes (1977). *Coronelismo: The Municipality and Representative Government in Brazil*. Cambridge: CUP.
- Malathronas, John (2003). *Brazil: Life, Blood, Soul*. Chichester: Summersdale.
- Martinez-Lara, Javier (1995). *Building Democracy in Brazil: The Politics of Constitutional Change*. Macmillan.
- Prado Júnior, Caio (1967). *The Colonial Background of Modern Brazil*. Los Angeles, CA: University of California Press.
- Schneider, Ronald (1995). *Brazil: Culture and Politics in a New Economic Powerhouse*. Boulder Westview.
- Skidmore, Thomas E. (1974). *Black Into White: Race and Nationality in Brazilian Thought*. Oxford: Oxford University Press.
- Wagley, Charles (1963). *An Introduction to Brazil*. New York, New York: Columbia University Press.
- *The World Almanac and Book of Facts: Brazil*. New York, NY: World Almanac Books. 2006.

External links

- Official Tourist Guide of Brazil (http://www.braziltour.com/)
- Brazilian Federal Government (http://www.brasil.gov.br/?set_language=en)
- Chief of State and Cabinet Members (https://www.cia.gov/library/publications/world-leaders-1/world-leaders-b/brazil.html)
- Brazilian Institute of Geography and Statistics (http://www.ibge.gov.br/english/)
- Brazil (https://www.cia.gov/library/publications/the-world-factbook/geos/br.html) entry at *The World Factbook*
- Brazil (http://ucblibraries.colorado.edu/govpubs/for/brazil.htm) at *UCB Libraries GovPubs*
- Brazil (http://www.dmoz.org/Regional/South_America/Brazil/) at the Open Directory Project
- Country Profile (http://lcweb2.loc.gov/frd/cs/brtoc.html) from the U.S. Library of Congress (1997)
- Brazil travel guide from Wikitravel
- Video report on Brazil in 1961 (http://www.itnsource.com/shotlist//BHC_ITN/1961/10/12/X12106101/)
- OpenStreetMap has geographic data related to Brazil (http://www.openstreetmap.org/browse/relation/59470)

kbd:Бразил gag:Braziliya mrj:Бразили ltg:Brazileja xmf:ბრაზილია rue:Бразілія

Article Sources and Contributors

Sport_Club_Santos_Dumont *Source*: http://en.wikipedia.org/w/index.php?title=Sport_Club_Santos_Dumont *Contributors*: Carioca

Salvador,_Bahia *Source*: http://en.wikipedia.org/w/index.php?title=Salvador%2C_Bahia *Contributors*: !Silent, *drew, 08OceanBeach SD, 1297, 1oddbins1, A8UDI, Abberley2, Abhijitsathe, Affleck, Al Lemos, Alansohn, Aleph Infinity, Alexander507pty, Alvesfilho, Amicon, Amillar, Angenhariaus, Angr, Annebb11, Anomalocaris, Antipodean Contributor, ApprenticeFan, Arguru, Arosa, Arpingstone, Artefactual, Ary29, Auntof6, B, BD2412, Barticus88, Berger1, Bhadani, Billinghurst, Bobblehead, Bolivian Unicyclist, Bradv, Brossow, BuddyX, C010T3, C273, CRKingston, CambridgeBayWeather, Camw, Can't sleep, clown will eat me, Carcharoth, CavaloBranco, CesarB, Champsdfw, Chowbok, CoCoLumps, CoJaBo, Commander Keane, CommonsDelinker, Correionago, Corvus cornix, Cristiano Tomás, Danny, Dapsv, Darwinek, Davehi1, David Kernow, Davidwr, Dekimasu, Dentren, DerBorg, Dhum Dhum, Dickdock, Diegocosta, Digodf, Discospinster, Domaleixo, Dr. Blofeld, Dss971, DuendeThumb, EamonnPKeane, Edson Henrique Rosa Junior, Edson Rosa, ElfWarrior, EugeneZelenko, Evandrojr, Fabhcún, Fallschirmjäger, Fasouzafreitas, Fernando.webstrats, Flewis, Flink the blind hemophiliac, Floridianed, Foobar, Fratrep, Fsouza, Fvasconcellos, G. Capo, Gaius Cornelius, Garotoo, Geniac, GoingBatty, Graham87, Gramado, Greenshed, Grenzer22, Grey Shadow, GuilhermeSalgado, Gurchzilla, Haggen Kennedy, Hajor, Hateless, Hazelday, Heitor CJ, Helixweb, Hentzer, HiMyNameIsFrancesca, Historymike, HkCaGu, Hmains, Howcheng, Husond, IGreil, Infrogmation, Innv, Iridescent, Itakauser1, J.delanoy, JaGa, Jahiegel, JamesAM, Jao, Japanese Searobin, Jay1279, Jenblower, Jerzey Belle, JesseW, Jevansen, Jhendin, Joaomsoliveira, Joey80, JohnMink, Johnbibby, Jorge Stolfi, Joseph Solis in Australia, Jrk3150, Jtiagomdias, Jujutacular, Jusdafax, Juxt23, Kakofonous, Karl Dickman, Kateri.oneil, Klemen Kocjancic, Knightrunner, Kristof vt, Kukini, Kuru, LibStar, LilHelpa, LoserTalent, Lvklock, M4c0, MJCdetroit, Ma'ame Michu, Mactin, Magafuzula, Maniac18, Marc Venot, Marek69, Mareklug, Mbatist, Mbinebri, Mesnenor, Michaelbusch, Miguel Chong, Milaloli, Mild Bill Hiccup, Miller17CU94, Milton Stanley, Miq, Mr Accountable, Mr.Z-man, MrRhythm, Mufka, Muhandes, Napoleon Dynamite42, Nayumadehrafti, Neddyseagoon, Nick Number, Nightkey, Nilderson, Ninguém, Nixeagle, Nk, Notmyrealname, Octavio medina, Opinoso, Ospalh, Oxey89, Paulistanum, Peloneous, Philip Trueman, PiaH, Piano non troppo, Playclever, Pocket Rockets, Producaosp, R psleite, R'n'B, RafaAzevedo, Rafael1996sa, Rahlgd, Ramirez72, Randalllin, Raven in Orbit, Revolución, Reywas92, Rich Farmbrough, Rich257, Richardprins, Rickipedia127, Rodbrassa, Rodhullandemu, Rodrigogomespaixao, Rodssa, Ron asquith, Ronaldo, Roscelese, Rosecrans, Rusinho, S.K., Sagaciousuk, Sampa1974, Scheridon, Schoci, Scotthatton, Scriberius, Selachophile, Serkul, Sfoskett, ShelfSkewed, Sitenl, Skanter, Skarebo, Sluzzelin, Sonett72, Spacepotato, Spangineer, Spiesr, Stepheng3, Sting-fr, Stone, Swarm, Taamu, Talrias, Tauane, The bellman, Themfromspace, Thiagoreis leon, TimBentley, Timrollpickering, Tomer T, Toxicsquall, Tpbradbury, Tpsaraiva, TravelingFool, Travgrl, Twas Now, Uclopes, Udibi, Ugur Basak, Unyoyega, VITALLITY, Victor Lopes, Voyagerfan5761, WOSlinker, WereSpielChequers, West81, Wfgiuliano, Wik, WildWildBil, Wildhartlivie, William Avery, Wimt, Woohookitty, Writtenonsand, Xuxo, Xyzzyva, Yurov, Zemilideias, Zen Clark, Zidonuke, Zimzilabim, Δ, 1246 anonymous edits

Campeonato_Baiano *Source*: http://en.wikipedia.org/w/index.php?title=Campeonato_Baiano *Contributors*: Beto, Carioca, Djln, Ed g2s, Edwardx, Jmorrison230582, KnightRider, Ms2ger, Quicksilvre, 29 anonymous edits

Bahia *Source*: http://en.wikipedia.org/w/index.php?title=Bahia *Contributors*: *drew, 1297, AK Auto, Aadavalus, Abhijitsathe, Academic38, Adam Keller, Aec is away, Ahoerstemeier, Alexanderkahn, Alro, Altenmann, Amillar, Andre Engels, Andres, Andycjp, Angenhariaus, ApprenticeFan, Avaragado, Avocet2, Avsa, Backslash Forwardslash, Baldhur, Beemer69, Bentley4, Berton, Bezuidenhout, BilCat, Billinghurst, Bluemask, Bobblehead, BrunoSL, BryanG, Btl, Cacetudo, Caiaffa, Caioipiau, CambridgeBayWeather, Can't sleep, clown will eat me, Caponer, Captain panda, Cesar Moura, Chanheigeorge, Chrism, Clemmy, Clew Cringle, CoJaBo, Colonies Chris, CommonsDelinker, Ctjf83, Cybercobra, D6, DO'Neil, Danny, Davehi1, Davidlakota, Davidwr, Dekimasu, Dhum Dhum, DjZ, Download, Drmies, Dyss, ESkog, Elekhh, Eplymesser, Epolk, Erianna, Fasouzafreitas, Felipe Menegaz, FisherQueen, Frankie816, Fsouza, Gadfium, Gaius Cornelius, Geniac, Good Olfactory, Grafen, Gramado, Grenzer22, Gsandi, Guilherme Paula, H L 78, Hagerman, Hentzer, Hephaestos, Hmains, Holliv, Hottentot, Identidade, Incornsyucopia, Infrogmation, InternationalHit2, Irregulargalaxies, Island, Isnow, Istanbuljohnm, Jab843, Jaume87, Jdb00, Jeppiz, Joaopais, Joseph Solis in Australia, Joy, Jrk3150, Jtir, Junnior.holanda, Jørdan, Keenan Pepper, Khoikhoi, Koyaanis Qatsi, Kwamikagami, Lightmouse, Lima, LoserTalent, Luizdl, MJCdetroit, Magnus Manske, Mandarax, Marek69, Markhurd, Martrau, Matthew hk, McLar eng, Mellery, Mereda, Michael brasil, Minnecologies, Missionary, Modulatum, Morwen, NAB 9892, Naniwako, NeilN, Niteowlneils, Notmyrealname, Nuttycoconut, OldakQuill, Open2universe, Opinoso, P. S. F. Freitas, P4k, Palmalouca, Paradaxarada, Paul Richter, Pcb21, PedroAguiar, PeterHuntington, Phn229, Pilotguy, Pinnecco, Plasticspork, Plastikspork, Pocket Rockets, Pollinator, Polylerus, Ptah, the El Daoud, Puckly, QuartierLatin1968, Radon210, Ramirez72, Raven in Orbit, Redhill54, Redlentil, Rich Farmbrough, Rich257, Rjensen, Rjwilmsi, Robert Weemeyer, Rodriguerus, Roger.lee, SQL, Scanlan, Serkul, Sitenl, Skanter, Slawojarek, Solipsist, Spellmaster, Stan Shebs, Stifle, Stogie10, Suhardian, Sundberg, Supervaca, Template namespace initialisation script, Tesi1700, Tevildo, Tom Radulovich, Toussaint, Una Smith, Uncle Dick, Underlying lk, Unyoyega, UtherSRG, Vanka5, Vdjj1960, Vsmith, WOSlinker, Websterwebfoot, Whosyourjudas, Wknight94, Wwoods, Yabsa, Yurov, Zoe, 392 anonymous edits

Alberto_Santos-Dumont *Source*: http://en.wikipedia.org/w/index.php?title=Alberto_Santos-Dumont *Contributors*: 7, 84user, A D Monroe III, AHands, Ahoerstemeier, Akradecki, AlainV, Alfadelta1525, Altzinn, Amon Barros, Anna Lincoln, Anonymous from the 21st century, Architeuthis, August10, Augustojd, Awesome1111, AxelBoldt, BD2412, Bag shoots, Bagunceiro, BaomoVW, Bastique, Bazem, Bbsrock, Benwing, Bepp, BilCat, Billthekid77, Blimpguy, Blondeonblonde2, BlueMoonlet, Bluejay52, Bobblewik, Brandon97, Brian0918, Bxistos, Bzuk, C08040804, CanDo, Canglesea, Canuck85, Capmo, Carlossuarez46, Chienlit, Chris the speller, Chrisboote, Chrispounds, Clarityfiend, Cloretti2, Colonies Chris, CommonsDelinker, Crum375, Cyfal, D1tempo, D6, DARTH SIDIOUS 2, DO'Neil, Dabean, Danceswithzerglings, Dantadd, Dark Shikari, DeadEyeArrow, DeivsonPrescovia, Delirium, DerHexer, Dezillio, Diego, DisillusionedBitterAndKnackered, Dominic, DonFB, Dpotop, Dr. Dan, DragonflySixtyseven, Dreadstar, Driftwoodzebulin, Dsmdgold, Dudeman5685, ElBenevolente, Elisabeth P. Waugaman, Elisabeth Waugaman, Elizi, Ellmist, Emilemil, EncMstr, Epbr123, Eurosong, Evlekis, FJM, Felipe Menegaz, Filhodapuc, Frankskey, Funandtrvl, Gadfium, Gaius Cornelius, GeeJo, Gikü, Good Olfactory, Graham87, GrahamBould, Greenshed, Grenzer22, Greyengine5, Grr, Grummerx, Gunter, Guy Harris, Harold f, Harryzilber, Hasannur, Herostratus, Hmains, Horst, Howcheng, Hu12, Huangdi, IceDragon64, Infrogmation, J.delanoy, Jarbru, Jeffdaro, Jezhotwells, Jggouvea, Jgroub, Jmcc150, Joefaust, John, John of Reading, JohnnyMrNinja, Jonas Mur, JonathanDP81, Jorge Stolfi, JorgeGG, Joseph Solis in Australia, Joserbn, Joshua Scott, Jun Nijo, Junglejimgems, JuniperisCommunis, KTo288, Kansan, Karmafist, KateikyoushiHitmanReborn, Keegeo3, Kman543210, Kozuch, Krauss, Kristbg, Kumioko, Kungfuadam, Kylu, Leandrod, Leandropls, Lecen, Leon7, LeonardoRob0t, Leondumontfollower, Lewiscb, LeyteWolfer, Lezebre, Lightmouse, Ling.Nut, Lipeca, Loukinho, Lsloan, Luizdl, MAAGNESE, MK, Madchester, Marlonbraga, Martinense, Marx Gomes, Maximus Rex, McSly, Mdchachi, Mernen, Mets501, Mgaletti, Michael David, MiguelMunoz, Mike Selinker, Mintguy, Mirror Vax, Missionary, Modulatum, Morven, Moshe Constantine Hassan Al-Silverburg, Mostsigbit, Mouchoir le Souris, MrRhythm, Mrmdog, Mrzero, Mtruax, Nathanww, Nelbr, Noob09, Nrh, Nwerneck, Oggers408, Omalako, Opinoso, Osias, Paracel63, Paul August, Per Honor et Gloria, Petri Krohn, Phil Boswell, PhilKnight, Philip Trueman, Pibwl, Pigsonthewing, Pinnecco, Pokeronskis, Purplefeltangel, Q1443, Quadell, Quase, Rams118, Rawdatasmith, Renzo Grosso, Richard Arthur Norton (1958-), Rjsc, Rjwilmsi, Rlandmann, Rmhermen, RodC, Rothorpe, Rsabbatini, Rstratta, Rtdrury, Rui Gabriel Correia, Sam Hocevar, Samwb123, Sesel, Sherurcij, Skysmith, Snowmanradio, Sobolewski, Stephenb, Strategy No 2, Sunderland06, Supersexyspacemonkey, Szum, Tcascardo, Ted Wilkes, Tfine80, The Bushranger, The PIPE, The Thing That Should Not Be, TheGerm, TheLongTone, Thumperward, Tillman, Tjmayerinsf, Tonsa, Tony1, Trekphiler, Uerba, Undead warrior, V! The Vile, Velella, WOSlinker, Walterego, Wednesday Next, WhisperToMe, Wildie, Wmahan, Woodnwheel, Wotnow, YellowMonkey, Yugo4k, Zwilson14, Δ, 579 anonymous edits

Brazil *Source*: http://en.wikipedia.org/w/index.php?title=Brazil *Contributors*: (:Julien:), -- April, -unicycle-pro-, 1234r00t, 123Hedgehog456, 159753, 172, 200.204.171.xxx, 21655, 2help, 322095480th, 334a, 4twenty42o, 5 albert square, 99econ, A Werewolf, A.Z., A8UDI, AA, ACSE, AV3000, Aaron Einstein, Aaron Schulz, Aaron045, Aaronbrick, Aaronthered, Abductive, Aboydvd, Abreuzinho, Abu badali, Abueno97, Abyssal, Academic38, Acer, Achangeisasgoodasa, Acolston, Acs4b, AdamFouracre, Adashiel, Addicted04, Addlertod05, AdeMiami, Adolphus79, Adrian, Adrian Robson, Aerolitz, Aervanath, Aesopian, Aesopos, Aeusoes1, AfC, Affleck, Afiler, Afluent Rider, Agil, Ahoerstemeier, Ahuskay, Ahwaz, Aivazovsky, Aj2121, Ajwitney, Akanemoto, Akradecki, Al-Andalus, Alan Liefting, Alan lyra, Alan27, Alanbcao, Alansohn, Alberto msr, Alcguerreiro, AlefZet, Alex houlbrook, Alex-ridgeway, AlexBrainer, AlexCovarrubias, Alexander Domanda, Alexcetera, Alexinc9, AlexiusHoratius, Alexwcovington, Algarb, Alihadji, Alison, AliveFreeHappy, Aliyevramin, Allstar86, Alvarolima, Alvaroludolf, Amakuru, Amarao, Amazonien, Amdsweb, Amgreg, AmigoDoPaulo, Amnesia the dark descent 2010, Anakay, Anarchist92, Andre Engels, Andrecury, AndrewWTaylor, Andrewlp1991, Andrewpmk, Andrewudstraw, Andrwsc, Andy Marchbanks, Angela, Angelo De La Paz, Angie Y., Angr, Angusmclellan, Anis93, Anonymous from the 21st century, Antandrus, Anthony, Anthonyd3ca, Antipodean Contributor, Antonio Basto, Antt296, ApS Camper, Aquintero82, Aramaicus, Ard77, Arendedwinter, Arialblack, Ariedartin, Armpit1999, Arpingstone, Art LaPella, Arthur Rubin, Arthurhenriquemsm, Artur 55, Asabovesobellow, Asdfghjklasdfjk, Assab, Astronautics, Asyndeton, Atick22, AuburnPilot, Aude, Augusto f. arruda fontes, Auréola, Australia boy, Autocracy, Autoerrant, Autolykos2, Avala, Aventinus, Avenue, Avicennasis, Axeman89, Azips, BGManofID, BSTIMELESS, Bagunceiro, Baliok, Banana04131, Barek, Barfooz, Baristarim, BarkerJr, Barneca, BarretB, Barryob, Bart133, Barticus88, Bazonka, Bcnviajero, Bcoverson, Beatrijs9, Beeblebrox, Beelzebubs, Behemoth, Bein04, Belache, Ben Ben, Bender235, Bendono, BenettonHuhera, Bensci54, Benson85, Bepp, Betacommand, Beyond silence, Bgwwlm, Bidabadi, Bility, Bill Thayer, Bill37212, Billgunyon, Billscottbob, Billybobdoodle, Birdmessenger, Biruitorul, Bishop^, Bj the pimp, Bjarki S, Bkell, Blackable2323, Blake24, Blamed, Blaxthos, Blessthishouse, Bletch, Blizzardstep0, Bloodshedder, Blue520, Blueyez941, Bmil, Bob bobato, Bobblewik, Bobo192, Bogdan, Bolivian Unicyclist, Bomac, Bombs Bombs Away!, Bomfim, Bookandcoffee, Boomshadow, Bowei Huang, Bownser, Bpiereck, BradBeattie, Brasilturismo, Brazil4Linux, BrazilBoy1996, Brazilian101, Brazillianideas, Brazzer, Brazzillover, Bremen, BrendelSignature, Brian0918, Brianski, Brion VIBBER, Brisvegas, Brother Officer, Broux, Browni1992, Brutaldeluxe, Bryan Derksen, BryanWhite5858, Btball, Buaidh, Buchanan-Hermit, Bucksburg, BuddyX, Bull Market, Bumm13, Burbridge92, Burgaqueen14, Buttered Bread, Bwabes, CALR, CEBR, CMoosey, Cactus.man, Cadr, Caesar, Califate123!, Calmer Waters, Caltas, Calton, Cambalachero, CambridgeBayWeather, Camenzind, Can't sleep, clown will eat me, Canadian Eclat, CanadianLinuxUser, Canderson7, Caniago, CanisRufus, Cantus, Capmo, Caribbean H.Q., Cariello, Carioca, Carlaude, Carlon, Carlosguitar, Carnildo, CasanovaUnlimited, Catstamford, Ccmfarias, Cdc, Ceilican, Celestra, Centrx, Ceres1251, Cesar Moura, CesarB, Ceyockey, Chafis, Chamdarae, Chan Han Xiang, Chanting Fox, Charlesblack, CharlotteWebb, Chase me ladies, I'm the Cavalry, Chaser, Che829, Cheiro de lysoform, Chensiyuan, ChiPHeaD, Chicchick, Chicocvenancio, Chinneeb, Chipmunkdavis, Chowhotin, Chrislk02, Christoff2k7, Chromega, Chubberi, Ciacchi, Ciao 90, CieloEstrellado, Cillmore, Civil Engineer III, CjGenius, Ck3001, Ckatz, ClaudioMB, Claygate, Cloretti, Cloretti2, Cmaster360, Cmdrbond, Cmdrjameson, Codex Sinaiticus, Coleecer, Colipon, Colofac, Colonel Tom, Colonies Chris, CommonsDelinker, Confiteordeo, Connormah, Conscious, Constihill, Conversion script, Cool Stuff Is Cool, Cool boy 96, CordeliaNaismith, Corvus13, CrazySlyHawk, Crazypersonbb, Credema, Creedence, Cripipper, Crisco 1492, Cromag, Crownjewel82, Crum375, Crònica, Cs-wolves, Cup22, Curps, Cvalente, Cwebb4000, Cyapt81, Cyberanto, Cybershore, D6, DCGeist, DDerby, DE MAGIC PICKLE, DH85868993, DMac, DMeyering, DMorpheus, DNewhall, DO'Neil, DTC, Daffy100, Daftpunker88,

Article Sources and Contributors 91

Dalillama, Damirgraffiti, Danga, Daniel Callegaro, Daniel G Rego, Daniel J. Leivick, DanielCD, DanielVonEhren, Danny, Dannyha2007, Dantadd, Darkwind, Darry2385, David Johnson, David Kernow, David Liuzzo, Davidprior, Dawei20, Dazcue, Dbaker22, Dburgoszarazo, Dc freethinker, Dcandeto, DeJuanio, DeadEyeArrow, Deborahhosen, Debresser, Deckchair, Deflective, Dekimasu, Delbadger2, Delirium, Delldot, DeltaQuad, Dendodge, Dennis Brown, Der Falke, DerBorg, DerHexer, Derek.cashman, Deus Ex, Deviathan, Dewet, Deyyaz, Dfdc, Dfrg.msc, Dheerajrao, Dhp1080, Diana Prallon, Diego UFCG, Diegowarrior, Dina, Dinosaur puppy, Dinosaurdarrell, Diogo sfreitas, Dipper2, Discospinster, Dispenser, Distal24, Djheini, Djibouti.Djibouti, Dkamouflage, Dlohcierekim, Doc Tropics, DocRocks1, Doctorage, Docu, Dogaroon, Dogfacebob, Doidimais Brasil, Dolovis, Dominictimms, Dominik78, Domino theory, Doorwerth, DopefishJustin, DorisH, Doubleplusunbig, Doug Johnson, Dpecego, Dpmelo, Dppowell, Dqndqnlol, Dr Aaij, Dr Nascimento, Dr. Miasma, Dr. Zaret, Dr.K., Dragonflysixtynine, Dragonitedude09, Dralwik, Dravecky, Drbug, Dreaded Walrus, Drewrau, Drhou, Drilnoth, Drmies, Drumguy8800, Dsloan, Dsvyas, Dtrielli, Dub8lad1, Dude112887, Dumb13d0r3, Duncachinno, Durnthalerk, Durrus, Dwrcan, DylanW, Dynamicknowledge28, Dysmorodrepanis, Dzeanis, Dzianis, Dálmata, Dúnadan, Dýrlegur, E Pluribus Anthony, ERcheck, ESkog, Eagle4000, Eallik, Eamaral, EamonnPKeane, Earthlyreason, Eastjame, Eastlaw, EatAlbertaBeef, EconomistBR, Ed g2s, Eddabed, Eddie6705, Edelmar Schneider, Edgeweb, Edisoncm, Editore99, Edivorce, Edson Rosa, Eduardo Sellan III, Edward, Effisk, Egel, Egil, Eiler7, Eisnel, Ejk81, El C, Electionworld, Elekhh, Elektrik Shoos, Elium2, Ella Plantagenet, Elockid, ElockidAlternate, Eltl 312, Elvenearth, Emblazoned, Emc2, Emmster, Emperorbma, Emsox, Emyne, EncycloPetey, English rosy, Enoma14, Epbr123, Epicadam, Epolk, Equilibrial, EricSerge, Erinfish, Eroica, Esas, Escape Orbit, Escoria, Eskimoinsane, Esn, EternamenteAprendiz, Etxrge, Euchiasmus, EugeneZelenko, Eurosong, Evenfiel, Everyking, Everytime, Evil Monkey, Excelsior Deo, Excirial, Exert, Exlibris, Exukvera, Eyeintheskye, Ezadarque, Ezeu, FF2010, Fabiorosa, Falcon8765, Falsedef, Fastestdogever, FatTux, FayssalF, Feddhicks, Fel Arthur, Felipaudi, Felipe Menegaz, Felipepiresdias, Fenice, Fermion, Fernandoe, FiP, Fieldday-sunday, Filhodapuc, FilipeS, Finneganw, Finngall, FireOcean, Fireaxe888, Firstorm, FisherQueen, Fito, FlamingSilmaril, Flatterworld, FloNight, Flobthelog, Floorwalker, Flyer1994, Flyguy649, Flyingidiot, Flávio Paiva F1, Footballfan190, Fourthords, Foxcloud, Franz weber, Freakified, Freakofnurture, Freakıfied, Fredrik, Frenchifri, FreplySpang, Frietjes, Fry1989, Frymaster, Fsolda, Funnybunny, Funnyhat, Furries, Fuzheado, Fvasconcellos, GAVINkeddie11, GHe, GSoledade, Gabrielsouza15, Gaf.arq, Gaff, Gaius Cornelius, Galoveri, Ganunu, Gareth E Kegg, Garima661, Gary King, Garzo, Gasheadsteve, Gaybobrando, Gazen 91, Gazpacho, Gbuch, Gdavidp, Geni, Geniac, GeoffreyVS, Gfoley4, Gggh, Ghaly, Giampersa, Giftlite, Giggy, Gilliam, Gimferrer, Ginkgo100, Giorgioz, Giraffedata, Giro720, Glauberfc, Glenn, Gnarlyjim, Gogo Dodo, Gohan341, Golbez, Good Olfactory, Goodbyebean, GorillaWarfare, Goro87, Gotrl, Gpak360, Grace E. Dougle, Gracenotes, GraemeL, Grafen, Graham, Graham87, GrahamTM, GreatWhiteNortherner, Green Giant, Grendelkhan, Grenzer22, Greyhood, Grick, Gringojack, Grosplant, Ground Zero, Grsz11, Grunt, Gryffindor, Guanaco, Guanaco152003, Guff Brooking, Guiestevam, Guilherme Paula, Gurch, Gustavo Siqueira, Gwguffey, Gzkn, Gzornenplatz, H0ttamale2, HP465, Haakon, Haaqfun, Hadal, Haham hanuka, Hairy Dude, Hajor, Hanike, Harburg, Harrisles, Harryboyles, Harrypotter90, Hasek is the best, Hayden120, Hchasestevens, Hdante, Hdt83, Hector.C.Jorge, Heelmijnlevenlang, Heezy, HeikoEvermann, Heitor CJ, Hektor, Helloguy123, Hempfel, Henning Makholm, HenryLi, Hentzer, Hibernian, Highvale, Higorspario, HisSpaceResearch, Hmains, Hmdwgf, Hoary, Holden 2, Homerjay, Honbicot, Honeyhucket, HoriaG, Hoshie, Hu12, Hughcharlesparker, Hugoreis, Huhsunqu, Hullaballoo Wolfowitz, IANVS, ILHI, IOUANAME666, Ian6650, Ibrox, IceDragon64, Idaltu, Idontknow610, Ief, Igorgonzola, Ikh, Ilikemilktoo, Illegitimate Barrister, Illexsquid, Ilunga Shibinda, Imastraightg, Improv, InShaneee, Indech, Infrogmation, InglesIngles, InspectorTiger, Interestingstuffadder, Ionutzmovie, Iqbaal, Iridescent, Irrypride, Isak11, IsamaraCruciol, Isinbill, Italiano111, Italo Svevo, Itanesco, Iudaeus, Iv1607, IveGotTV, Ixfd64, J Crow, J Di, J.Wright, J04n, JERRKOWA, JForget, JG-Guilherme12, JJJJust, JLogan, JStewart, Jaburc, Jack Thundercliffe, Jack10, Jackl, JackoAUS, JackofOz, Jagged 85, Jajafe, JakeNichols, Jalada, JamesR, Jamespenido, Jameston, Jamirabastos, Janiovj, Jaranda, Jarjarbinks10, Jasonjmartin, Jasperdiablo, Jb849, Jbob360, Jcra, Jdc360, JeanKorte, Jebba, JedOs, Jeeny, Jeff G., Jeff3000, Jeffhoy, Jeffrey O. Gustafson, Jeffreymcmanus, Jenmen, Jerbbson, JeremyA, Jeronimo, Jerry1234567890, Jerrygarciuh, Jerryseinfeld, JesseW, Jesusmariajalisco, Jetekus, Jewbask, Jgk168421, Jh51681, Jhendin, Jhowcs, Jiang, JimWae, Jimmy Slade, Jimtaip, Jindanbo, Jjm9090, Jk2q3jrklse, Jlpspinto, Jmartinezot, Jmlk17, Jmorrison230582, JoSePh, JoanneB, Joao, Joaopais, Joaosac, Joelalvarado, Joevicentini, Johanneum, John, John of Reading, John254, Johnluisocasio, Johnny Jane, Johnpseudo, Jojhutton, Jomig, Jon33, Jonas Mur, Jonathan Fernando, Jonildosb, Jorge Stolfi, JorgeGG, JorgePeixoto, Jorunn, Jose.armando.jeronymo, Joseph Solis in Australia, JoshuaD1991, Jossi, José Henrique Campos, Jpeob, Jsferreira, Jsnruf, Jsydave, Jtir, Ju98 5, Juan A. Malo de Molina, Jughead28773, Julinho, Jumentodonordeste, Jurema Oliveira, Jusdafax, JustAGal, Justice for All, Jvatoledo, Jvhertum, K50 Dude, KNM, KVDP, Kaasje, Kaihoku1, Kairos, Kaiserble, Kakofonous, Kalemguzeli, Kanatonian, Kardrak, Karl Dickman, Karolvs, Katefan0, Katydidit, KaylendraDawn, Keegan, Keelm, Keilana, Keitei, Kelisi, Kelvinc, Kemm@ig.com.br, Kenmcfa, Kevinkor2, Kharker, Khoikhoi, Khukri, Kiensvay, Kievz, Killer1587, Kimon, King Toadsworth, King of Hearts, KingTT, Kingpin13, Kintetsubuffalo, Kinu, Kkm010, Klop79, Km905, Kman543210, Kmusser, Kneuronak, KnowledgeOfSelf, Knutux, Ko'oy, Koavf, Korath, Korean alpha for knowledge, Kosunen, Kotakkasut, Kotniski, Koyaanis Qatsi, Kozuch, Kozushi, Kr1st1deejay97, KramerNL, Krich, Kross, Kukini, KumfyKittyKlub, Kungfuadam, Kurogawa, Kurt is nutz, Kuru, Kurykh, Kusb, Kusma, Kuzaar, Kwamikagami, L Kensington, LA2, Lacobrigo, Lahuwm, Lampman, Lankiveil, Lapaz, Larkosh, Laubz83, Laurens-af, Lcawte, Leandrod, Lecen, Lefterispapi, Leo Stedile, Leoadec, Leonardi, Leonardo Alves, Leonardomio, Lesfer, Leszek Jańczuk, Leuko, Levineps, Lewiscb, Lexi Marie, Lguipontes, LibLord, Libertariandude, Licor, Liftarn, Lifung, Lightmouse, Lights, Limongi, Ling.Nut, Linkspamremover, Little Mountain 5, Localzuk, Lockesdonkey, Lokodd, LonerXL, Looxix, Lord Dandy, LordLancaster, Los rios, Losangeleslive, Loserjay10, Losttiiee, Lotje, Lp crn, Lssilva, LucasEllerNYC, Luckyj, Ludger1961, Luizdl, Lukeprizer, Lulu Margarida, Luna Santin, Lunarboy, Lunkwill, Lusci, Lussier, Lyricmac, MCBastos, MER-C, MFago, MIT Trekkie, MJCdetroit, MSGJ, MaGioZal, Macgreco, MackSalmon, MadCrazyMaster, Madden, Madjohnflint, Maelnuneb, Maester mensch, Magafuzula, Magister Mathematicae, Mahanga, Majorly, Malerin, Malhonen, Malleus Fatuorum, Malo, Man vyi, Mandolinface, Manoel.canova, Maokart444, Marcio.gregory, Marco Neves, Marcos Elias de Oliveira Júnior, Marcus Qwertyus, Mareeah, Mareino, Marek69, Mareklug, Marekzp, Marianocecowski, Mario Profaca, Mario777Zelda, Mariordo, MarkGallagher, MarkSutton, MarshalN20, Martarius, Martimsaintive, MartinHarper, Martinwilke1980, Marx Gomes, Massari, Master Bigode, Master of Puppets, Maszanchi, Materialscientist, Mateus RM, Mateuszica, Mattbr, Matthew Desjardins, Matthew Yeager, Mattiecat, Maximus Rex, Maxtremus, Maxwell's Daemon, Maxxicum, Mayakovsky5, Mazca, Mbakkel2, Mbello82, Mberbert, Mboverload, McDogm, McSly, Mchasewhittemore, Mdob, Mecanismo, Meegs, Meesham, Mephiston999, Mermaid from the Baltic Sea, Merovingian, Mesgul82, Mesoso2, Metallion, Methcub, Methnor, MetroPlayer, Mets501, Meursault2004, Mfa fariz, Mhsb, Mic, Michaelmas1957, Michaelrccurtis, Mickey gfss2007, Mickeykozzi, Midgrid, MigraineBigBoy, Mike Rosoft, MikeAllen, MikeBruski, Mikep2008a, Mikespedia, Mild Bill Hiccup, MinnesotanConfederacy, Missionary, Missspencer06, MisterJ88, Mitsuhirato, Mjpieters, Mlepori, Mm40, Mocu, ModelFish, ModestMouse2, Modi mode, Moeron, Mohmoe, Momo san, Moncrief, MontseBL, Moofinluvr, Mopcwiki, Mori Riyo, Moriori, Morrad, Mouramoor, Mp2171998, Mr Adequate, Mr. Anon515, Mr. Lefty, Mr.Z-man, Mr666, MrBojanglesNY, MrPMonday, MrRhythm, Mrcometpar, Mrkarate, Mschel, Mschiffler, Msikma, Mtmelendez, Mulad, Mulder416, Munci, Mushroom, Mwanner, Mxcatania, Mxn, Myanw, Myleslong, MysteryDog, Mário, N5iln, NHRHS2010, NJOrlando, NYDCSP, Nahallac Silverwinds, Nakon, Nate1481, Nathan Johnson, Naveenbm, NawlinWiki, Neko-chan, Netoholic, Neutrality, Nhgill, Nichalp, Nick Taylor, Nicksss93, Night w, Nightmarelh, Nightstallion, Nihiltres, Nihonjoe, Nikai, Nilderson, Nillanilla3ee, Ninguém, Nivisec, Nivix, Nk, Nmiwil, NoahLevitt, NormanEinstein, Norway1, Nosbig, Notchcode, Notheruser, Novaguy1968, Novowalace, NuclearVacuum, Nurg, Nyttend, OOODDD, Obonicus, Octane, Oda Mari, Odilamaria, Odin's Eye, Ohnoitsjamie, Oleg Alexandrov, Oli1944, Olivier, Ollie carlo, Omicronpersei8, Omnibus, Omnipotentjefe, OneGuy, OneWorld22, Oneearth, Onlim, Onopearls, Onorem, Opelio, OpiniónCiudad, Opinoso, Optimist on the run, Oreo Priest, OrgasGirl, Ospalh, Owess, Oxymoron83, Ozzyprv, P3navy04, PDH, PMLF, Pablosaraiva, Packtsardines, Page Up, Paine Ellsworth, Palapa, Paleorthid, Pandacomics, Paplvcraker12, Paranhos.fabio, Parserpractice, Patrasmentium, PatríciaR, Patstuart, PaulQuagliata, Pcgomes, Pedreco, PedroPVZ, Pedrovitorh2, Peer V, Pekaje, Pepper, Pepperfield69, Peter Horn, Peter Winnberg, PeterisP, Pgk, Pgunn, Pharaoh of the Wizards, Phil5329, Philbuck222, Phileas, Philip Trueman, Phillip J, Philosopher, Piernodoyuna, Pigman, Pikolas, Pilim, Pilotguy, Pilotnews, Pinethicket, Piniricc65, Pinkville, Pinnecco, Piperh, Pishogue, Plankhead, Plm209, Pngin lvr, Poecilia Reticulata, Pointillist, Pol098, Polaron, Poli, Polylerus, Popcorn12212, Porcher, Portillo, Potosino, Pras, Predictor92, PrestonH, Prince Paul of Yugoslavia, Prodego, Prumpf, PseudoSudo, Pspprogo, Psy guy, Ptah, the El Daoud, Puddington, Puertorico1, Pularoid, Purple Paint, Purpleturple, Qtoktok, Quadell, QueenStupid, Questchest, Quiensabe, Quintote, Quissamã, Quite vivid blur, Qutezuce, Qxz, R Lee E, R'n'B, R-Joe, R9tgokunks, RG2, RHB, RJHigginson, RVD, RaCha'ar, Rabindra Baral, Radiant!, RadiantRay, RadioKirk, RafaAzevedo, RafaelG, Rafavargas, Rafazero27, Rahlgd, Rainmaker, Rairun, Rajnr, Ral315, Ramalha Soares, Ramesh Chandra, Ramirez72, Ran, Random user 8384993, Raprat0, Rarelibra, RaseaC, Rastrudwick, Ratherhaveaheart, Ratzd'mishukribo, Ratzer, Raven in Orbit, Raylu, RazorICE, Rbras75, Rcerque1, Rdsmith4, Reaper Eternal, Recnilgiarc, Red Director, Red Thrush, RedWolf, Rednblu, Redstorm77, Redtricycle, Redux, Reedy, Reflynn, Reggy123, Reguard, Reisio, Renato Caniatti, Rettetast, RexNL, Reywas92, Reztip, Rfredian, Rhamphorynchus, Riana, Ricardo Carneiro Pires, Ricardo257, Ricardo630, Rich Farmbrough, Richardcavell, Richarddd, Richerman, Richi, Richmond Falls, Rick Block, RickK, Ricklongo, Ricky81682, Ricky@36, Rickyy, RicoCorinth, Ridow, Rillian, Rinconsito, Ringbang, Rjwilmsi, Rkt2312, RoadTrain, Robbert12, RobertG, Robertgreer, Robertomalancini, Robocoder, RockerTux, Rockford1963, Rockinthisjoint, Rockmysock, Rockslave, RodC, Rodak1, Rodrigo123456, RodrigoBr, Rodrigogomesonetwo, Rodrigogomespaixao, Roke, Romanm, RonaldoBr, Ronark, Rooozter, RoscoeDK, Roxanna samii, RoyBoy, Royalguard11, Rsabbatini, Rubywhite, Rudjek, RunOrDie, Russell Brown, Rwickss, Ryan Roos, Ryanjunk, Rydra Wong, Ryulong, S, SJP, STGM, SWAdair, Sade, SahirShah, Salmar, Sam Hocevar, SamEV, Samiamhapyfeet, Sammocool, Samohad, Sampi, Samwb123, Sanbeg, Sandhuswarn, Sandstein, Sango123, Sanmartin, Sardanaphalus, Savant13, Sayden, Scarface1991, Schepop, Scheridon, Schieese, Schoen, Schzmo, Scipius, Sciurinæ, Scott14, Scuppers1, Sdornan, Seaphoto, Seatonsk8r, Seb az86556, Sebastiankessel, Secfan, Secretlondon, Sectori, Segho, Sekwanele 2, Selerz, Sentinel, SephyXIII, Ser Amantio di Nicolao, Serblood, Sevenlee, SgtFlem, Shadow Scythe of Strongbadia?!, Shaggorama, Shakam, Shakko (usurped), Shanel, Shanes, Shangrilaista, Shantetrey, Sheppa28, Shiva0x007, Shoeofdeath, Shroudan, SidP, Sidasta, Siddhant, SieberNewsAt7, Sietse Snel, Silivrenion, Silly rabbit, Silvafilho, Silverclaw12, SimonP, Simonmatt1100, SiobhanHansa, Sir Nicholas de Mimsy-Porpington, Sir Vicious, Siroxo, Sirwhiteout, Sitenl, Sj, Sjakkalle, Skanter, Skavuska, Skinnyweed, Slakr, Sligocki, Slippered sleep, Slippknotryan, Sloman, Slowking Man, Smark2, SmartGuy, Smertios, Smsagro, Sn0wflake, Snigbrook, Sodicadl, Solitude, Some jerk on the Internet, Sometimes somethings, Sonjaaa, Sophie means wisdom, Sord freak8, Soulja nyn3, Southamerica2010, SpaceFlight89, Spamhuntert, Sparks1979, Spellcast, Spinoff, SpookyMulder, SpuriousQ, Spylab, Squamate, Squamben15, SqueakBox, Squids and Chips, Squirepants101, Srikeit, Srini81, Ssolbergj, Sspecter, St.daniel, StAnselm, Staj44, Star-of-David92, Star2589, Starghost, Starionwolf, Staxringold, Stcknight13, Stealthjacko, Steel, Stemonitis, Stephanobeghini, Stephen e nelson, Stephenb, Stephenthompson, Stevey7788, Stifynsemons, Stormy56, Straatmeester, Strait, Strikerforce, Stroppolo, Struway, Studgilpin, Sturunner, Styath, SuPERLman, Summerswirl 1 a, Sumskate111, Sunderland06, Supaman89, SuperTycoon, Superbeatles, Supertask, Surtsicna, Suruena, Susan Capetinga, Svato, Swatjester, Szil66, T, TAG-A-b10, TJ Spyke, TKD, TUF-KAT, Tabletop, Taconinja5000, Tacv, Taelus, Taksim25, Talalpa, Talon Artaine, Tanet, Tangotango, Tanketai, Tanketz, Taospark, Tarret, TastyCakes, TastyPoutine, Tatarian, Tatterfly, Tawker, Taxman, Tbhotch, TeaDrinker, Tedder, Teketime, Telemachus.forward, Tellyaddict, Template namespace initialisation script, Terence, Tevildo, Tfine80, ThaGrind, The Fat Guy, The Fear, The Fuher Of Putkas, The Gaon, The High Fin Sperm Whale, The Hybrid, The Lake Effect, The Moose, The Ogre, The One True Fred, The Rambling Man, The Thing That Should Not Be, The Transhumanist, The Universe Is Cool, The ed17, The idiot, The undertow, The-G-Unit-Boss, TheGrza, ThePedanticPrick, TheProject, TheRanger, Thebombzaway, Theda, Thedemonhog, Thehelpfulone, Thenewestdoctorwho, Therequiembellishere, Thetaylor310, Thetraytiger, Thewallowmaker, Thewisetortoise, Thiagoreis leon, Thobbyas, Thomas Weriden, Thornhilboy, Tibullus, Tide rolls, TigerShark, Tiggie, Tim1357, TimBentley, Timmy317, Timwi, Tinhorao, Tintazul, TintininLisbon, Tioperci, Tired time, Tisiacs, Titoxd, Tjcloo11, Tjl1128, Tjpob, Tmoulin2, To lead you in the summer to join the black parade!, Toanvungtau, Tobby72, Tobias Conradi, Tobizz, Tobyc75, TodorBozhinov, Togamoos, Tohd8BohaithuGh1, Tommyladder, Tomsega, Tomtefarbror, Tomyumgoong, Tony Sidaway, Tony1, Tonyboy27, Tonyfv, Toonarmy01, Topbanana, Tornadou, Torqueing, Toussaint, Tpbradbury, Trabalhosgv, Trampton, Trasman, Travelbird, Tregoweth, TriTertButoxy, Trinten, Triplexxx56, Troelz, Trödel, Tsf, Tterrag, Tugaworld, Tumtum95, TutterMouse, Twerbrou, Two Bananas, Twsx, Tx207, Tycoonjack, Tyler fog, Tyrantbigbird, Tyrol5, Ucanlookitup, Uchiha 7, Uconn boy, Ucucha, Udibi, Uerba, Ufwuct, Ugen64, Ularevalo98, Uli82, Ultimate Destiny, Ultimus, Ultranol, Uncle Dick, Underlying lk, UniReb, Uniemelk, Uniqueuponhim, Untouchable777, UrsoBR, Uruguayo, Utcursch, Uxejn, V4R, V6g3h7, VampWillow, Van helsing, VandalCruncher, Vaniac, Vaniba12, Vanished User 1004, Vanka5,

Vapmachado, Vaquero100, Vardion, Varlaam, Vary, Vbs, Veertlte, Vega84, Vegaskeeper, Velho, Ventur, VerasGunn, VerdaTeo, Versageek, Vertigo200, VeryVerily, Vgoradia, Victor12, Victorfri, Viewfinder, Vikingstad, Viktordb, VincentG, Vinegar, Violadamore, Vir, Virgule82, Virtual Cowboy, VitaleBaby, Vivaldi4Stagioni, Vivaperucarajo, Vivekdse, VolatileChemical, Voldemortuet, Vsion, Vsmith, Vtguy4242, Vzbs34, Waggers, Walrasiad, Waltloc, Ward3001, Warfvinge, Warofdreams, WarthogDemon, WaterMelon7, Wavehunter, Wavelength, Wayward, Weakopedia, Welsh, Wengero, Werdan7, Westphalen, Wet Putka, Wetman, Weyes, WhisperScreamIshowIscream, WhisperToMe, Who, Wicojrpr, Widefield, Wik, WikHead, Wiki alf, WikiHendrik, Wikidan7, Wikiperuvian, Wikiscribe, Wildfox, Wildie, Wilkolad, Will Beback, Wimt, Windofkeltia, Wine Guy, Wingwangwo, Wiplar, Wk muriithi, Wknight94, Wkoide, Wlegro, Wlmh65, Wmahan, Wolffystyle, WolfgangFaber, Woohookitty, Ww2, XGustaX, Xandi, Xariana, Xatlasm, Xbows, Xezbeth, Xiong Chiamiov, Xuxo, Xyzzyva, Yacht, Yahel Guhan, Yamamoto Ichiro, Yansa, Yardena, Yasis, YellowMonkey, YgorCoelho, Yodaki, Yorkist, Yossiea, YoungSpinoza, Youssefsan, Ypacaraí, Z.E.R.O., Zahid Abdassabur, Zakuragi, Zap Rowsdower, Zappa711, Zarcadia, Zarxos, Zeca valeiro, Zero Gravity, Zhonghuo, Zhub, Zink Dawg, Zoe, ZooFari, Zoomzoom, Zscout370, Zvar, Zvn, ZwickauDeluxe, Zzuuzz, Zzyzx11, Île flottante, बोधिचित्त, , , 4515 anonymous edits

Image Sources, Licenses and Contributors

File:Montagem Salvador.jpg *Source*: http://en.wikipedia.org/w/index.php?title=File:Montagem_Salvador.jpg *License*: unknown *Contributors*: User:Heitor C. Jorge
File:Bandeira de Salvador.svg *Source*: http://en.wikipedia.org/w/index.php?title=File:Bandeira_de_Salvador.svg *License*: unknown *Contributors*: Luan, Nethunter, Sitenl
File:Brasão de Salvador.jpg *Source*: http://en.wikipedia.org/w/index.php?title=File:Brasão_de_Salvador.jpg *License*: unknown *Contributors*: uploaded
File:Bahia Municip Salvador.svg *Source*: http://en.wikipedia.org/w/index.php?title=File:Bahia_Municip_Salvador.svg *License*: unknown *Contributors*: Darlan P. de Campos
file:Brazil location map.svg *Source*: http://en.wikipedia.org/w/index.php?title=File:Brazil_location_map.svg *License*: unknown *Contributors*: Little Savage, Mizunoryu, NordNordWest, Shadowxfox, Vinícius Nery, 1 anonymous edits
File:Red pog.svg *Source*: http://en.wikipedia.org/w/index.php?title=File:Red_pog.svg *License*: unknown *Contributors*: Anomie
File:Flag of Brazil.svg *Source*: http://en.wikipedia.org/w/index.php?title=File:Flag_of_Brazil.svg *License*: unknown *Contributors*: Anomie
Image:Bandeira da Bahia.svg *Source*: http://en.wikipedia.org/w/index.php?title=File:Bandeira_da_Bahia.svg *License*: unknown *Contributors*: User:E2m
File:Sunset in Barra - Salvador, Brazil.JPG *Source*: http://en.wikipedia.org/w/index.php?title=File:Sunset_in_Barra_-_Salvador,_Brazil.JPG *License*: unknown *Contributors*: User: Hentzer
File:Solar Ferrão fachada 2008.jpg *Source*: http://en.wikipedia.org/w/index.php?title=File:Solar_Ferrão_fachada_2008.jpg *License*: unknown *Contributors*: User:André Koehne
File:Salvadoratnight.JPG *Source*: http://en.wikipedia.org/w/index.php?title=File:Salvadoratnight.JPG *License*: unknown *Contributors*: User:Rossignol008
File:Campo Grande ssa.jpg *Source*: http://en.wikipedia.org/w/index.php?title=File:Campo_Grande_ssa.jpg *License*: unknown *Contributors*: Antônio Cruz dos Santos Júnior
File:Skyline of Salvador, Brazil.jpg *Source*: http://en.wikipedia.org/w/index.php?title=File:Skyline_of_Salvador,_Brazil.jpg *License*: unknown *Contributors*: User:Hentzer
File:Farol da Barra - Salvador, Brazil.JPG *Source*: http://en.wikipedia.org/w/index.php?title=File:Farol_da_Barra_-_Salvador,_Brazil.JPG *License*: unknown *Contributors*: User: Hentzer
File:Centenário Avenue - Salvador, Brazil.jpg *Source*: http://en.wikipedia.org/w/index.php?title=File:Centenário_Avenue_-_Salvador,_Brazil.jpg *License*: unknown *Contributors*: (User: Hentzer). Original uploader was Hentzer at en.wikipedia
File:Lindo Sol em Plataforma.jpg *Source*: http://en.wikipedia.org/w/index.php?title=File:Lindo_Sol_em_Plataforma.jpg *License*: unknown *Contributors*: Tiago Celestino from Bahia, Brazil
File:Avtancredoneves23012011.JPG *Source*: http://en.wikipedia.org/w/index.php?title=File:Avtancredoneves23012011.JPG *License*: unknown *Contributors*: User:Sitenl
File:Salvador BA.jpg *Source*: http://en.wikipedia.org/w/index.php?title=File:Salvador_BA.jpg *License*: unknown *Contributors*: FlickreviewR, Heitor CJ
File:Cruzeiros no Porto de Salvador.jpg *Source*: http://en.wikipedia.org/w/index.php?title=File:Cruzeiros_no_Porto_de_Salvador.jpg *License*: unknown *Contributors*: Agecom Bahia from Bahia/Brasil
File:Salvador-CCBY-5.jpg *Source*: http://en.wikipedia.org/w/index.php?title=File:Salvador-CCBY-5.jpg *License*: unknown *Contributors*: joquerollo , modified by Fulviusbsas
File:Marco da Fundação, Salvador (3).jpg *Source*: http://en.wikipedia.org/w/index.php?title=File:Marco_da_Fundação,_Salvador_(3).jpg *License*: unknown *Contributors*: Luan
File:Elevador Lacerda Salvador Bahia.jpg *Source*: http://en.wikipedia.org/w/index.php?title=File:Elevador_Lacerda_Salvador_Bahia.jpg *License*: unknown *Contributors*: Felipe Menegaz, FlickreviewR, Luan, Marku1988
File:Salvador shopping goumert.jpg *Source*: http://en.wikipedia.org/w/index.php?title=File:Salvador_shopping_goumert.jpg *License*: unknown *Contributors*: User:Murilokurteforro
File:Yatch Club da Bahia 2.jpg *Source*: http://en.wikipedia.org/w/index.php?title=File:Yatch_Club_da_Bahia_2.jpg *License*: unknown *Contributors*: Luan
File:Callitrichidaes in the Catholic University of Salvador, Brazil.JPG *Source*: http://en.wikipedia.org/w/index.php?title=File:Callitrichidaes_in_the_Catholic_University_of_Salvador,_Brazil.JPG *License*: unknown *Contributors*: Hentzer
File:Faculdade medicina bahia.jpg *Source*: http://en.wikipedia.org/w/index.php?title=File:Faculdade_medicina_bahia.jpg *License*: unknown *Contributors*: André Koehne, Jurema Oliveira
File:Salvador-CCBY-2.jpg *Source*: http://en.wikipedia.org/w/index.php?title=File:Salvador-CCBY-2.jpg *License*: unknown *Contributors*: joquerollo
File:Forte s diogo vista aerea salvador.jpg *Source*: http://en.wikipedia.org/w/index.php?title=File:Forte_s_diogo_vista_aerea_salvador.jpg *License*: unknown *Contributors*: Fundação Cultural Exército Brasileiro
File:Anchieta Pelourinho Cyark.jpg *Source*: http://en.wikipedia.org/w/index.php?title=File:Anchieta_Pelourinho_Cyark.jpg *License*: unknown *Contributors*: CyArk
File:Salvador-JesuitChurch4-CCBY.jpg *Source*: http://en.wikipedia.org/w/index.php?title=File:Salvador-JesuitChurch4-CCBY.jpg *License*: unknown *Contributors*: fernando_dallacqua
File:IURD Salvador - A Casa da Moeda.jpg *Source*: http://en.wikipedia.org/w/index.php?title=File:IURD_Salvador_-_A_Casa_da_Moeda.jpg *License*: unknown *Contributors*: Samory Santos from Salvador, Brazil
File:Cyark salvador cross.jpg *Source*: http://en.wikipedia.org/w/index.php?title=File:Cyark_salvador_cross.jpg *License*: unknown *Contributors*: DuendeThumb, 1 anonymous edits
File:TerceirosSFrancisco-Salvador-CCBYSA.jpg *Source*: http://en.wikipedia.org/w/index.php?title=File:TerceirosSFrancisco-Salvador-CCBYSA.jpg *License*: unknown *Contributors*: Bruno Girin
File:Feijoada 01.jpg *Source*: http://en.wikipedia.org/w/index.php?title=File:Feijoada_01.jpg *License*: unknown *Contributors*: Jurema Oliveira, Kintetsubuffalo, Ras67, Zephynelsson Von
File:Bloco da Capoeira, Circuito Campo Grande 2008.jpg *Source*: http://en.wikipedia.org/w/index.php?title=File:Bloco_da_Capoeira,_Circuito_Campo_Grande_2008.jpg *License*: unknown *Contributors*: Fabio Rodrigues Pozzebom/ABr uploaded
File:View over Harbour Area from Hotel Arthemis - Salvador - Brazil.jpg *Source*: http://en.wikipedia.org/w/index.php?title=File:View_over_Harbour_Area_from_Hotel_Arthemis_-_Salvador_-_Brazil.jpg *License*: unknown *Contributors*: User:Adam63
File:Carniaval Salvador Bahia Brazil 1997.jpg *Source*: http://en.wikipedia.org/w/index.php?title=File:Carniaval_Salvador_Bahia_Brazil_1997.jpg *License*: unknown *Contributors*: User:Floridianed
File:Bloco da camisinha circuito Campo Grande Salvador.jpg *Source*: http://en.wikipedia.org/w/index.php?title=File:Bloco_da_camisinha_circuito_Campo_Grande_Salvador.jpg *License*: unknown *Contributors*: Foto:Antônio Cruz/ABr
File:Barra-Ondina no carnaval de Salvador em 2008.jpg *Source*: http://en.wikipedia.org/w/index.php?title=File:Barra-Ondina_no_carnaval_de_Salvador_em_2008.jpg *License*: unknown *Contributors*: Foto: Fabio Pozzebom/ABr
File:Gabinete Português de Leitura 2.jpg *Source*: http://en.wikipedia.org/w/index.php?title=File:Gabinete_Português_de_Leitura_2.jpg *License*: unknown *Contributors*: User:Luan
File:Bloco dos Bonecões no Pelourinho.jpg *Source*: http://en.wikipedia.org/w/index.php?title=File:Bloco_dos_Bonecões_no_Pelourinho.jpg *License*: unknown *Contributors*: Fábio Rodrigues Pozzebom/ABr uploaded
File:Sala de embarque do Aeroporto Luiz Eduardo Magalhães 3.JPG *Source*: http://en.wikipedia.org/w/index.php?title=File:Sala_de_embarque_do_Aeroporto_Luiz_Eduardo_Magalhães_3.JPG *License*: unknown *Contributors*: Fábio Pozzebom/ABr uploaded
File:A Marina de Salvador.jpg *Source*: http://en.wikipedia.org/w/index.php?title=File:A_Marina_de_Salvador.jpg *License*: unknown *Contributors*: Samory Santos from Salvador, Brazil
File:Salvador Metro.png *Source*: http://en.wikipedia.org/w/index.php?title=File:Salvador_Metro.png *License*: unknown *Contributors*: User:Hentzer
File:Linha Verde2.jpg *Source*: http://en.wikipedia.org/w/index.php?title=File:Linha_Verde2.jpg *License*: unknown *Contributors*: Claus Bunks aka Afrobrasil on flickr
File:Praia da Barra na véspera do Carnaval 2008 de Salvador.jpg *Source*: http://en.wikipedia.org/w/index.php?title=File:Praia_da_Barra_na_véspera_do_Carnaval_2008_de_Salvador.jpg *License*: unknown *Contributors*: Fabio Pozzebom/ABr uploaded
File:Edificios na Av. Tancredo Neves.jpg *Source*: http://en.wikipedia.org/w/index.php?title=File:Edificios_na_Av._Tancredo_Neves.jpg *License*: unknown *Contributors*: Samory Santos from Salvador, Brazil
File:Beach of Farol da Barra - Salvador, Brazil.JPG *Source*: http://en.wikipedia.org/w/index.php?title=File:Beach_of_Farol_da_Barra_-_Salvador,_Brazil.JPG *License*: unknown *Contributors*: User: Hentzer
File:Estádio Manoel Barradas Vitória.jpg *Source*: http://en.wikipedia.org/w/index.php?title=File:Estádio_Manoel_Barradas_Vitória.jpg *License*: unknown *Contributors*: Carol Garcia / AGECOM
File:Arenafontenova.png *Source*: http://en.wikipedia.org/w/index.php?title=File:Arenafontenova.png *License*: unknown *Contributors*: User:Engenheiro Leandro
File:Victoria's Secret models visit Guantanamo, December 2007.jpg *Source*: http://en.wikipedia.org/w/index.php?title=File:Victoria's_Secret_models_visit_Guantanamo,_December_2007.jpg *License*: unknown *Contributors*: photo by Navy Petty Officer 3rd Class William Weinert
File:Flag of the United States.svg *Source*: http://en.wikipedia.org/w/index.php?title=File:Flag_of_the_United_States.svg *License*: unknown *Contributors*: Anomie

Image Sources, Licenses and Contributors

File:Seal of Los Angeles, California.svg *Source*: http://en.wikipedia.org/w/index.php?title=File:Seal_of_Los_Angeles,_California.svg *License*: unknown *Contributors*: w:User:MysidMysid
File:Flag of California.svg *Source*: http://en.wikipedia.org/w/index.php?title=File:Flag_of_California.svg *License*: unknown *Contributors*: w:en:User:DevinCookDevin Cook
File:Flag of Portugal.svg *Source*: http://en.wikipedia.org/w/index.php?title=File:Flag_of_Portugal.svg *License*: unknown *Contributors*: User:Nightstallion
File:Crest of Lisboa.svg *Source*: http://en.wikipedia.org/w/index.php?title=File:Crest_of_Lisboa.svg *License*: unknown *Contributors*: User:Leovilok
File:AGH.png *Source*: http://en.wikipedia.org/w/index.php?title=File:AGH.png *License*: unknown *Contributors*: Brian Boru, Knorrepoes, Lusitana, Magul, Zeorymer
File:Flag of the Azores.svg *Source*: http://en.wikipedia.org/w/index.php?title=File:Flag_of_the_Azores.svg *License*: unknown *Contributors*: User:Tonyjeff
File:CSC.png *Source*: http://en.wikipedia.org/w/index.php?title=File:CSC.png *License*: unknown *Contributors*: Sérgio Horta
File:Flag of Benin.svg *Source*: http://en.wikipedia.org/w/index.php?title=File:Flag_of_Benin.svg *License*: unknown *Contributors*: User:Gabbe, User:SKopp
File:Flag of Spain.svg *Source*: http://en.wikipedia.org/w/index.php?title=File:Flag_of_Spain.svg *License*: unknown *Contributors*: Anomie
File:Escudo de Pontevedra.svg *Source*: http://en.wikipedia.org/w/index.php?title=File:Escudo_de_Pontevedra.svg *License*: unknown *Contributors*: User:SanchoPanzaXXI
File:Flag of Galicia.svg *Source*: http://en.wikipedia.org/w/index.php?title=File:Flag_of_Galicia.svg *License*: unknown *Contributors*: Pedro A. Gracia Fajardo
File:Flag of Cuba.svg *Source*: http://en.wikipedia.org/w/index.php?title=File:Flag_of_Cuba.svg *License*: unknown *Contributors*: see below
File:Escudo de la Habana.svg *Source*: http://en.wikipedia.org/w/index.php?title=File:Escudo_de_la_Habana.svg *License*: unknown *Contributors*: User:HansenBCN
File:Flag of Italy.svg *Source*: http://en.wikipedia.org/w/index.php?title=File:Flag_of_Italy.svg *License*: unknown *Contributors*: Anomie
File:Sciacca-Stemma.png *Source*: http://en.wikipedia.org/w/index.php?title=File:Sciacca-Stemma.png *License*: unknown *Contributors*: Attilios, Magul
File:Sicilian Flag.svg *Source*: http://en.wikipedia.org/w/index.php?title=File:Sicilian_Flag.svg *License*: unknown *Contributors*: User:Klone123, User:Thyes
File:Flag of the People's Republic of China.svg *Source*: http://en.wikipedia.org/w/index.php?title=File:Flag_of_the_People's_Republic_of_China.svg *License*: unknown *Contributors*: User:Denelson83, User:SKopp, User:Shizhao, User:Zscout370
File:.jpg *Source*: http://en.wikipedia.org/w/index.php?title=File:.jpg *License*: unknown *Contributors*: Yanglei8310
File:Escudo de Miami.svg *Source*: http://en.wikipedia.org/w/index.php?title=File:Escudo_de_Miami.svg *License*: unknown *Contributors*: User:Rastroj
File:Flag of Florida.svg *Source*: http://en.wikipedia.org/w/index.php?title=File:Flag_of_Florida.svg *License*: unknown *Contributors*: Awg1010, Dbenbenn, Denelson83, DenghiùComm, Dzordzm, Ebyabe, Fry1989, Himasaram, Homo lupus, Hystrix, Madden, Mattes, Nightstallion, Pumbaa80, Reach Out to the Truth, Reuvenk, Rocket000, Vantey, Zscout370, 13 anonymous edits
File:Soccerball current event.svg *Source*: http://en.wikipedia.org/w/index.php?title=File:Soccerball_current_event.svg *License*: unknown *Contributors*: User:Anomie, User:Davidgothberg, User:Pumbaa80
File:Bandeira da Bahia.svg *Source*: http://en.wikipedia.org/w/index.php?title=File:Bandeira_da_Bahia.svg *License*: unknown *Contributors*: User:E2m
File:Brasão da Bahia.png *Source*: http://en.wikipedia.org/w/index.php?title=File:Brasão_da_Bahia.png *License*: unknown *Contributors*: User:André Koehne
File:Brazil State Bahia.svg *Source*: http://en.wikipedia.org/w/index.php?title=File:Brazil_State_Bahia.svg *License*: unknown *Contributors*: Raphael Lorenzeto de Abreu
File:Cachoeira da fumaça 2.jpg *Source*: http://en.wikipedia.org/w/index.php?title=File:Cachoeira_da_fumaça_2.jpg *License*: unknown *Contributors*: r m
File:Chapada diamantina - ba.jpg *Source*: http://en.wikipedia.org/w/index.php?title=File:Chapada_diamantina_-_ba.jpg *License*: unknown *Contributors*: r m
File:Salvador Sao Marcelo fort from sea 2.jpg *Source*: http://en.wikipedia.org/w/index.php?title=File:Salvador_Sao_Marcelo_fort_from_sea_2.jpg *License*: unknown *Contributors*: User:Sting
File:BonfimSalvador-CCBY.jpg *Source*: http://en.wikipedia.org/w/index.php?title=File:BonfimSalvador-CCBY.jpg *License*: unknown *Contributors*: Tatiana Sapateiro
File:Vista Jequié.jpg *Source*: http://en.wikipedia.org/w/index.php?title=File:Vista_Jequié.jpg *License*: unknown *Contributors*: Ivo Leandro
File:Embarcadero ocaso.jpg *Source*: http://en.wikipedia.org/w/index.php?title=File:Embarcadero_ocaso.jpg *License*: unknown *Contributors*: User:Immersia
File:Usina Hidreletrica de Sobradinho-BA.jpg *Source*: http://en.wikipedia.org/w/index.php?title=File:Usina_Hidreletrica_de_Sobradinho-BA.jpg *License*: unknown *Contributors*: Glauco Umbelino from Moro em Belo Horizonte, Brasil
File:O Aeroporto de Ilhéus - Jorge Amado, Ilhéus, Bahia, Brasil.jpg *Source*: http://en.wikipedia.org/w/index.php?title=File:O_Aeroporto_de_Ilhéus_-_Jorge_Amado,_Ilhéus,_Bahia,_Brasil.jpg *License*: unknown *Contributors*: Carlos Mendonça
File:Morro1.jpg *Source*: http://en.wikipedia.org/w/index.php?title=File:Morro1.jpg *License*: unknown *Contributors*: Claus Bunks aka Afrobrasil on flickr
File:Igrejinha de Porto Seguro.jpg *Source*: http://en.wikipedia.org/w/index.php?title=File:Igrejinha_de_Porto_Seguro.jpg *License*: unknown *Contributors*: tiago araujo from Minas Gerais, Brasil
File:Vale do Pati.jpg *Source*: http://en.wikipedia.org/w/index.php?title=File:Vale_do_Pati.jpg *License*: unknown *Contributors*: Samory Santos from Salvador, Brazil
File:Prainha.JPG *Source*: http://en.wikipedia.org/w/index.php?title=File:Prainha.JPG *License*: unknown *Contributors*: User:FlaviaC
File:Colégio Estadual Thales de Azevedo.jpg *Source*: http://en.wikipedia.org/w/index.php?title=File:Colégio_Estadual_Thales_de_Azevedo.jpg *License*: unknown *Contributors*: Luan, Zacarias
File:Reitoria uefs.jpg *Source*: http://en.wikipedia.org/w/index.php?title=File:Reitoria_uefs.jpg *License*: unknown *Contributors*: UEFS
File:Pelourinho, Salvador.jpg *Source*: http://en.wikipedia.org/w/index.php?title=File:Pelourinho,_Salvador.jpg *License*: unknown *Contributors*: Bruno Girin uploaded
File:Bahia transportes.png *Source*: http://en.wikipedia.org/w/index.php?title=File:Bahia_transportes.png *License*: unknown *Contributors*: User:André Koehne
File:UnebVI.jpg *Source*: http://en.wikipedia.org/w/index.php?title=File:UnebVI.jpg *License*: unknown *Contributors*: User:André Koehne
File:Alberto Santos Dumont 02.jpg *Source*: http://en.wikipedia.org/w/index.php?title=File:Alberto_Santos_Dumont_02.jpg *License*: unknown *Contributors*: unknown
File:Assinatura do Santos Dumont 2.gif *Source*: http://en.wikipedia.org/w/index.php?title=File:Assinatura_do_Santos_Dumont_2.gif *License*: unknown *Contributors*: FML, Pikolas, 1 anonymous edits
File:Alberto Santos Dumont .jpg *Source*: http://en.wikipedia.org/w/index.php?title=File:Alberto_Santos_Dumont_.jpg *License*: unknown *Contributors*: "GEO HUM" (anonymous)
File:Sd num6 rounding tower.jpg *Source*: http://en.wikipedia.org/w/index.php?title=File:Sd_num6_rounding_tower.jpg *License*: unknown *Contributors*: Original uploader was Blimpguy at en.wikipedia
File:Aida-1903.jpg *Source*: http://en.wikipedia.org/w/index.php?title=File:Aida-1903.jpg *License*: unknown *Contributors*: Jack1956, Nunh-huh, 1 anonymous edits
File:Santos - Nov12 1906.jpg *Source*: http://en.wikipedia.org/w/index.php?title=File:Santos_-_Nov12_1906.jpg *License*: unknown *Contributors*: AnRo0002, Cirt, Duch.seb, KTo288, Mu, Sherurcij, Werneuchen
File:Alberto Santos Dumont flying the Demoiselle (1909).jpg *Source*: http://en.wikipedia.org/w/index.php?title=File:Alberto_Santos_Dumont_flying_the_Demoiselle_(1909).jpg *License*: unknown *Contributors*: User:Andrew M. Vachin
File:Le Petit Journal Santos Dumont 25 Novembre 1906.jpg *Source*: http://en.wikipedia.org/w/index.php?title=File:Le_Petit_Journal_Santos_Dumont_25_Novembre_1906.jpg *License*: unknown *Contributors*: Collective work
File:Wk000002.jpg *Source*: http://en.wikipedia.org/w/index.php?title=File:Wk000002.jpg *License*: unknown *Contributors*: Albertomos, FML, KTo288, Michael Romanov, Morio, Mu
File:House of Santos-Dumont Petropolis.jpg *Source*: http://en.wikipedia.org/w/index.php?title=File:House_of_Santos-Dumont_Petropolis.jpg *License*: unknown *Contributors*: Lucio Paiva
File:Alberto Santos-Dumont bust -near Brazilian Embassy, Washington, D.C., USA-26Aug2006.jpg *Source*: http://en.wikipedia.org/w/index.php?title=File:Alberto_Santos-Dumont_bust_-near_Brazilian_Embassy,_Washington,_D.C.,_USA-26Aug2006.jpg *License*: unknown *Contributors*: dbking from Washington, DC
File:santosdumonticecream.jpg *Source*: http://en.wikipedia.org/w/index.php?title=File:Santosdumonticecream.jpg *License*: unknown *Contributors*: Original uploader was Karmafist at en.wikipedia
File:Coat of arms of Brazil.svg *Source*: http://en.wikipedia.org/w/index.php?title=File:Coat_of_arms_of_Brazil.svg *License*: unknown *Contributors*: Brazilian Government
File:National Seal of Brazil (color).svg *Source*: http://en.wikipedia.org/w/index.php?title=File:National_Seal_of_Brazil_(color).svg *License*: unknown *Contributors*: User:Tonyjeff
File:Brazil (orthographic projection).svg *Source*: http://en.wikipedia.org/w/index.php?title=File:Brazil_(orthographic_projection).svg *License*: unknown *Contributors*: User:Ssolbergj
Image:Speakerlink.svg *Source*: http://en.wikipedia.org/w/index.php?title=File:Speakerlink.svg *License*: unknown *Contributors*: Woodstone. Original uploader was Woodstone at en.wikipedia
File:Meirelles-primeiramissa2.jpg *Source*: http://en.wikipedia.org/w/index.php?title=File:Meirelles-primeiramissa2.jpg *License*: unknown *Contributors*: User:Tetraktys

Image Sources, Licenses and Contributors

File:Independência ou Morte.jpg *Source*: http://en.wikipedia.org/w/index.php?title=File:Independência_ou_Morte.jpg *License*: unknown *Contributors*: CommonsDelinker, Dantadd, Dornicke, Lecen, Limongi, Lycaon, Picture Master, Pikolas, Raeky, Rocket000, Stigmj, Tetraktys, Tonyjeff, Zephynelsson Von, Ö, 2 anonymous edits

File:Pelourinho.jpg *Source*: http://en.wikipedia.org/w/index.php?title=File:Pelourinho.jpg *License*: unknown *Contributors*: Dantadd, Darwinius, G.dallorto, Juiced lemon, Jurema Oliveira, Ssasantos, , 1 anonymous edits

File:Americo-avai.jpg *Source*: http://en.wikipedia.org/w/index.php?title=File:Americo-avai.jpg *License*: unknown *Contributors*: Bukk, Dornicke, Lecen, Picture Master, Pikolas, Tetraktys, Vearthy, 3 anonymous edits

File:Revolução de 1930.jpg *Source*: http://en.wikipedia.org/w/index.php?title=File:Revolução_de_1930.jpg *License*: unknown *Contributors*: Claro Jansson (1877-1954)

File:Inauguration of Luiz Inácio Lula da Silva in 2003.jpeg *Source*: http://en.wikipedia.org/w/index.php?title=File:Inauguration_of_Luiz_Inácio_Lula_da_Silva_in_2003.jpeg *License*: unknown *Contributors*: Marcello Casal Jr./ABr

File:Brazil topo.jpg *Source*: http://en.wikipedia.org/w/index.php?title=File:Brazil_topo.jpg *License*: unknown *Contributors*: Original uploader was Captain Blood at en.wikipedia

Image:Neve na SC-438 em São Joaquim.JPG *Source*: http://en.wikipedia.org/w/index.php?title=File:Neve_na_SC-438_em_São_Joaquim.JPG *License*: unknown *Contributors*: User:Sorin

Image:Recife-Boa-Viagem-Orla.jpg *Source*: http://en.wikipedia.org/w/index.php?title=File:Recife-Boa-Viagem-Orla.jpg *License*: unknown *Contributors*: Dantadd, Davidandrade, Sitenl

File:Anavilhanas1.jpg *Source*: http://en.wikipedia.org/w/index.php?title=File:Anavilhanas1.jpg *License*: unknown *Contributors*: Jason Auch from Calgary, Canada

File:Congresso Nacional.jpg *Source*: http://en.wikipedia.org/w/index.php?title=File:Congresso_Nacional.jpg *License*: unknown *Contributors*: Gribiche (Rob Sinclair)

File:Supreme Federal Court of Brazil.jpg *Source*: http://en.wikipedia.org/w/index.php?title=File:Supreme_Federal_Court_of_Brazil.jpg *License*: unknown *Contributors*: Rob Sinclair

File:Itamaraty.jpg *Source*: http://en.wikipedia.org/w/index.php?title=File:Itamaraty.jpg *License*: unknown *Contributors*: xenia antunes from Brasilia, Brazil

File:Brazil Labelled Map.svg *Source*: http://en.wikipedia.org/w/index.php?title=File:Brazil_Labelled_Map.svg *License*: unknown *Contributors*: Felipe Menegaz, Giro720, Guilherme Paula, TZ master, Ulamm

File:Continental Embraer 135.jpg *Source*: http://en.wikipedia.org/w/index.php?title=File:Continental_Embraer_135.jpg *License*: unknown *Contributors*: gab_744

File:Agriculture in Brazil.PNG *Source*: http://en.wikipedia.org/w/index.php?title=File:Agriculture_in_Brazil.PNG *License*: unknown *Contributors*: User:João Felipe C.S

File:Itaipu noche.JPG *Source*: http://en.wikipedia.org/w/index.php?title=File:Itaipu_noche.JPG *License*: unknown *Contributors*: User:Carlosbenitez80

File:Lnls.jpg *Source*: http://en.wikipedia.org/w/index.php?title=File:Lnls.jpg *License*: unknown *Contributors*: Onbox

File:BR116 Viaduto em Fortaleza.jpg *Source*: http://en.wikipedia.org/w/index.php?title=File:BR116_Viaduto_em_Fortaleza.jpg *License*: unknown *Contributors*: Francisco Marinho de Andrade

File:Aeroporto do recife.jpg *Source*: http://en.wikipedia.org/w/index.php?title=File:Aeroporto_do_recife.jpg *License*: unknown *Contributors*: Alphax, Andre bispo, Apalsola, J o, Mattes, 1 anonymous edits

File:Festuva.jpg *Source*: http://en.wikipedia.org/w/index.php?title=File:Festuva.jpg *License*: unknown *Contributors*: Danirossi

File:Museu da Língua Portuguesa.jpg *Source*: http://en.wikipedia.org/w/index.php?title=File:Museu_da_Língua_Portuguesa.jpg *License*: unknown *Contributors*: Marilane Borges

File:Machado-450.jpg *Source*: http://en.wikipedia.org/w/index.php?title=File:Machado-450.jpg *License*: unknown *Contributors*: Academia Brasileira de Letras.

File:Barnetta061115-01.jpg *Source*: http://en.wikipedia.org/w/index.php?title=File:Barnetta061115-01.jpg *License*: unknown *Contributors*: User:reto

File:Openstreetmap logo.svg *Source*: http://en.wikipedia.org/w/index.php?title=File:Openstreetmap_logo.svg *License*: unknown *Contributors*: OpenStreetMap

GNU Free Documentation License Version 1.2, November 2002 Copyright (C) 2000,2001,2002 Free Software Foundation, Inc. 59 Temple Place, Suite 330, Boston, MA 02111-1307 USA Everyone is permitted to copy and distribute verbatim copies of this license document, but changing it is not allowed.

0. PREAMBLE
The purpose of this License is to make a manual, textbook, or other functional and useful document "free" in the sense of freedom: to assure everyone the effective freedom to copy and redistribute it, with or without modifying it, either commercially or noncommercially. Secondarily, this License preserves for the author and publisher a way to get credit for their work, while not being considered responsible for modifications made by others. This License is a kind of "copyleft", which means that derivative works of the document must themselves be free in the same sense. It complements the GNU General Public License, which is a copyleft license designed for free software. We have designed this License in order to use it for manuals for free software, because free software needs free documentation: a free program should come with manuals providing the same freedoms that the software does. But this License is not limited to software manuals; it can be used for any textual work, regardless of subject matter or whether it is published as a printed book. We recommend this License principally for works whose purpose is instruction or reference.

1. APPLICABILITY AND DEFINITIONS
This License applies to any manual or other work, in any medium, that contains a notice placed by the copyright holder saying it can be distributed under the terms of this License. Such a notice grants a world-wide, royalty-free license, unlimited in duration, to use that work under the conditions stated herein. The "Document", below, refers to any such manual or work. Any member of the public is a licensee, and is addressed as "you". You accept the license if you copy, modify or distribute the work in a way requiring permission under copyright law. A "Modified Version" of the Document means any work containing the Document or a portion of it, either copied verbatim, or with modifications and/or translated into another language. A "Secondary Section" is a named appendix or a front-matter section of the Document that deals exclusively with the relationship of the publishers or authors of the Document to the Document's overall subject (or to related matters) and contains nothing that could fall directly within that overall subject. (Thus, if the Document is in part a textbook of mathematics, a Secondary Section may not explain any mathematics.) The relationship could be a matter of historical connection with the subject or with related matters, or of legal, commercial, philosophical, ethical or political position regarding them. The "Invariant Sections" are certain Secondary Sections whose titles are designated, as being those of Invariant Sections, in the notice that says that the Document is released under this License. If a section does not fit the above definition of Secondary then it is not allowed to be designated as Invariant. The Document may contain zero Invariant Sections. If the Document does not identify any Invariant Sections then there are none. The "Cover Texts" are certain short passages of text that are listed, as Front-Cover Texts or Back-Cover Texts, in the notice that says that the Document is released under this License. A Front-Cover Text may be at most 5 words, and a Back-Cover Text may be at most 25 words. A "Transparent" copy of the Document means a machine-readable copy, represented in a format whose specification is available to the general public, that is suitable for revising the document straightforwardly with generic text editors or (for images composed of pixels) generic paint programs or (for drawings) some widely available drawing editor, and that is suitable for input to text formatters or for automatic translation to a variety of formats suitable for input to text formatters. A copy made in an otherwise Transparent file format whose markup, or absence of markup, has been arranged to thwart or discourage subsequent modification by readers is not Transparent. An image format is not Transparent if used for any substantial amount of text. A copy that is not "Transparent" is called "Opaque". Examples of suitable formats for Transparent copies include plain ASCII without markup, Texinfo input format, LaTeX input format, SGML or XML using a publicly available DTD, and standard-conforming simple HTML, PostScript or PDF designed for human modification. Examples of transparent image formats include PNG, XCF and JPG. Opaque formats include proprietary formats that can be read and edited only by proprietary word processors, SGML or XML for which the DTD and/or processing tools are not generally available, and the machine-generated HTML, PostScript or PDF produced by some word processors for output purposes only. The "Title Page" means, for a printed book, the title page itself, plus such following pages as are needed to hold, legibly, the material this License requires to appear in the title page. For works in formats which do not have any title page as such, "Title Page" means the text near the most prominent appearance of the work's title, preceding the beginning of the body of the text. A section "Entitled XYZ" means a named subunit of the Document whose title either is precisely XYZ or contains XYZ in parentheses following text that translates XYZ in another language. (Here XYZ stands for a specific section name mentioned below, such as "Acknowledgements", "Dedications", "Endorsements", or "History".) To "Preserve the Title" of such a section when you modify the Document means that it remains a section "Entitled XYZ" according to this definition. The Document may include Warranty Disclaimers next to the notice which states that this License applies to the Document. These Warranty Disclaimers are considered to be included by reference in this License, but only as regards disclaiming warranties: any other implication that these Warranty Disclaimers may have is void and has no effect on the meaning of this License.

2. VERBATIM COPYING
You may copy and distribute the Document in any medium, either commercially or noncommercially, provided that this License, the copyright notices, and the license notice saying this License applies to the Document are reproduced in all copies, and that you add no other conditions whatsoever to those of this License. You may not use technical measures to obstruct or control the reading or further copying of the copies you make or distribute. However, you may accept compensation in exchange for copies. If you distribute a large enough number of copies you must also follow the conditions in section 3. You may also lend copies, under the same conditions stated above, and you may publicly display copies.

3. COPYING IN QUANTITY
If you publish printed copies (or copies in media that commonly have printed covers) of the Document, numbering more than 100, and the Document's license notice requires Cover Texts, you must enclose the copies in covers that carry, clearly and legibly, all these Cover Texts: Front-Cover Texts on the front cover, and Back-Cover Texts on the back cover. Both covers must also clearly and legibly identify you as the publisher of these copies. The front cover must present the full title with all words of the title equally prominent and visible. You may add other material on the covers in addition. Copying with changes limited to the covers, as long as they preserve the title of the Document and satisfy these conditions, can be treated as verbatim copying in other respects. If the required texts for either cover are too voluminous to fit legibly, you should put the first ones listed (as many as fit reasonably) on the actual cover, and continue the rest onto adjacent pages. If you publish or distribute Opaque copies of the Document numbering more than 100, you must either include a machine-readable Transparent copy along with each Opaque copy, or state in or with each Opaque copy a computer-network location from which the general network-using public has access to download using public-standard network protocols a complete Transparent copy of the Document, free of added material. If you use the latter option, you must take reasonably prudent steps, when you begin distribution of Opaque copies in quantity, to ensure that this Transparent copy will remain thus accessible at the stated location until at least one year after the last time you distribute an Opaque copy (directly or through your agents or retailers) of that edition to the public. It is requested, but not required, that you contact the authors of the Document well before redistributing any large number of copies, to give them a chance to provide you with an updated version of the Document.

4. MODIFICATIONS
You may copy and distribute a Modified Version of the Document under the conditions of sections 2 and 3 above, provided that you release the Modified Version under precisely this License, with the Modified Version filling the role of the Document, thus licensing distribution and modification of the Modified Version to whoever possesses a copy of it. In addition, you must do these things in the Modified Version: A. Use in the Title Page (and on the covers, if any) a title distinct from that of the Document, and from those of previous versions (which should, if there were any, be listed in the History section of the Document). You may use the same title as a previous version if the original publisher of that version gives permission. B. List on the Title Page, as authors, one or more persons or entities responsible for authorship of the modifications in the Modified Version, together with at least five of the principal authors of the Document (all of its principal authors, if it has fewer than five), unless they release you from this requirement. C. State on the Title page the name of the publisher of the Modified Version, as the publisher. D. Preserve all the copyright notices of the Document. E. Add an appropriate copyright notice for your modifications adjacent to the other copyright notices. F. Include, immediately after the copyright notices, a license notice giving the public permission to use the Modified Version under the terms of this License, in the form shown in the Addendum below. G. Preserve in that license notice the full lists of Invariant Sections and required Cover Texts given in the Document's license notice. H. Include an unaltered copy of this License. I. Preserve the section Entitled "History", Preserve its Title, and add to it an item stating at least the title, year, new authors, and publisher of the Modified Version as given on the Title Page. If there is no section Entitled "History" in the Document, create one stating the title, year, authors, and publisher of the Document as given on its Title Page, then add an item describing the Modified Version as stated in the previous sentence. J. Preserve the network location, if any, given in the Document for public access to a Transparent copy of the Document, and likewise the network locations given in the Document for previous versions it was based on. These may be placed in the "History" section. You may omit a network location for a work that was published at least four years before the Document itself, or if the original publisher of the version it refers to gives permission. K. For any section Entitled "Acknowledgements" or "Dedications", Preserve the Title of the section, and preserve in the section all the substance and tone of each of the contributor acknowledgements and/or dedications given therein. L. Preserve all the Invariant Sections of the Document, unaltered in their text and in their titles. Section numbers or the equivalent are not considered part of the section titles. M. Delete any section Entitled "Endorsements". Such a section may not be included in the Modified Version. N. Do not retitle any existing section to be Entitled "Endorsements" or to conflict in title with any Invariant Section. O. Preserve any Warranty Disclaimers. If the Modified Version includes new front-matter sections or appendices that qualify as Secondary Sections and contain no material copied from the Document, you may at your option designate some or all of these sections as invariant. To do this, add their titles to the list of Invariant Sections in the Modified Version's license notice. These titles must be distinct from any other section titles. You may add a section Entitled "Endorsements", provided it contains nothing but endorsements of your Modified Version by various parties--for example, statements of peer review or that the text has been approved by an organization as the authoritative definition of a standard. You may add a passage of up to five words as a Front-Cover Text, and a passage of up to 25 words as a Back-Cover Text, to the end of the list of Cover Texts in the Modified Version. Only one passage of Front-Cover Text and one of Back-Cover Text may be added by (or through arrangements made by) any one entity. If the Document already includes a cover text for the same cover, previously added by you or by arrangement made by the same entity you are acting on behalf of, you may not add another; but you may replace the old one, on explicit permission from the previous publisher that added the old one. The author(s) and publisher(s) of the Document do not by this License give permission to use their names for publicity for or to assert or imply endorsement of any Modified Version.

5. COMBINING DOCUMENTS
You may combine the Document with other documents released under this License, under the terms defined in section 4 above for modified versions, provided that you include in the combination all of the Invariant Sections of all of the original documents, unmodified, and list them all as Invariant Sections of your combined work in its license notice, and that you preserve all their Warranty Disclaimers. The combined work need only contain one copy of this License, and multiple identical Invariant Sections may be replaced with a single copy. If there are multiple Invariant Sections with the same name but different contents, make the title of each such section unique by adding at the end of it, in parentheses, the name of the original author or publisher of that section if known, or else a unique number. Make the same adjustment to the section titles in the list of Invariant Sections in the license notice of the combined work. In the combination, you must combine any sections Entitled "History" in the various original documents, forming one section Entitled "History"; likewise combine any sections Entitled "Acknowledgements", and any sections Entitled "Dedications". You must delete all sections Entitled "Endorsements".

6. COLLECTIONS OF DOCUMENTS
You may make a collection consisting of the Document and other documents released under this License, and replace the individual copies of this License in the various documents with a single copy that is included in the collection, provided that you follow the rules of this License for verbatim copying of each of the documents in all other respects. You may extract a single document from such a collection, and distribute it individually under this License, provided you insert a copy of this License into the extracted document, and follow this License in all other respects regarding verbatim copying of that document.

7. AGGREGATION WITH INDEPENDENT WORKS
A compilation of the Document or its derivatives with other separate and independent documents or works, in or on a volume of a storage or distribution medium, is called an "aggregate" if the copyright resulting from the compilation is not used to limit the legal rights of the compilation's users beyond what the individual works permit. When the Document is included in an aggregate, this License does not apply to the other works in the aggregate which are not themselves derivative works of the Document. If the Cover Text requirement of section 3 is applicable to these copies of the Document, then if the Document is less than one half of the entire aggregate, the Document's Cover Texts may be placed on covers that bracket the Document within the aggregate, or the electronic equivalent of covers if the Document is in electronic form. Otherwise they must appear on printed covers that bracket the whole aggregate.

8. TRANSLATION
Translation is considered a kind of modification, so you may distribute translations of the Document under the terms of section 4. Replacing Invariant Sections with translations requires special permission from their copyright holders, but you may include translations of some or all Invariant Sections in addition to the original versions of these Invariant Sections. You may include a translation of this License, and all the license notices in the Document, and any Warranty Disclaimers, provided that you also include the original English version of this License and the original versions of those notices and disclaimers. In case of a disagreement between the translation and the original version of this License or a notice or disclaimer, the original version will prevail. If a section in the Document is Entitled "Acknowledgements", "Dedications", or "History", the requirement (section 4) to Preserve its Title (section 1) will typically require changing the actual title.

9. TERMINATION
You may not copy, modify, sublicense, or distribute the Document except as expressly provided for under this License. Any other attempt to copy, modify, sublicense or distribute the Document is void, and will automatically terminate your rights under this License. However, parties who have received copies, or rights, from you under this License will not have their licenses terminated so long as such parties remain in full compliance.

10. FUTURE REVISIONS OF THIS LICENSE
The Free Software Foundation may publish new, revised versions of the GNU Free Documentation License from time to time. Such new versions will be similar in spirit to the present version, but may differ in detail to address new problems or concerns. See http://www.gnu.org/copyleft/. Each version of the License is given a distinguishing version number. If the Document specifies that a particular numbered version of this License "or any later version" applies to it, you have the option of following the terms and conditions either of that specified version or of any later version that has been published (not as a draft) by the Free Software Foundation. If the Document does not specify a version number of this License, you may choose any version ever published (not as a draft) by the Free Software Foundation. ADDENDUM: How to use this License for your documents To use this License in a document you have written, include a copy of the License in the document and put the following copyright and license notices just after the title page: Copyright (c) YEAR YOUR NAME. Permission is granted to copy, distribute and/or modify this document under the terms of the GNU Free Documentation License, Version 1.2 or any later version published by the Free Software Foundation; with no Invariant Sections, no Front-Cover Texts, and no Back-Cover Texts. A copy of the license is included in the section entitled "GNU Free Documentation License". If you have Invariant Sections, Front-Cover Texts and Back-Cover Texts, replace the "with...Texts." line with this: with the Invariant Sections being LIST THEIR TITLES, with the Front-Cover Texts being LIST, and with the Back-Cover Texts being LIST. If you have Invariant Sections without Cover Texts, or some other combination of the three, merge those two alternatives to suit the situation. If your document contains nontrivial examples of program code, we recommend releasing these examples in parallel under your choice of free software license, such as the GNU General Public License, to permit their use in free software.